VEILED VOICES

VEILED VOICES

Muslim Girls in Public Schools

Dr. Jawairriya Abdallah-Shahid

A.A., Broome Community College, 1993
B.S., SUNY Cortland, 1995
M.S., SUNY Cortland, 1997
Ed.D., Binghamton University, 2008

Library of Congress Control Number:		2010902708
ISBN:	Hardcover	978-1-4500-5301-3
	Softcover	978-1-4500-5300-6
	eBook	978-1-4500-5302-0

Print information available on the last page.

Rev. date: 06/26/2019

To order additional copies of this book, contact:
Xlibris
1-888-795-4274
www.Xlibris.com
Orders@Xlibris.com
586126

CONTENTS

ABSTRACT

The six Muslim female students in this study wear *hijab* (head scarf) and attend public schools. The methods of this qualitative study include interviews, direct observation and photographs. These veiled Muslim females experience a multitude of difficulties that derive from being noticeably different in comparison to the general school population. Their desire to assimilate into their educational environments while maintaining their Muslim identity is a major component of their educational experience. Feelings of alienation, stigma, embarrassment and identity concerns are included in the everyday lives of these students.

Using the efforts of Goffman (1961, 1963, 1967) and Atikinson, Morten & Sue (1998) allows for the examination of both sociological and psychological perspectives relevant to adolescent Muslim females that wear hijab in the United States attending public schools. A historical overview of the origins of hijab, and the Muslim teachings regarding hijab are explained. The purpose is to provide an understanding of why these students veil. The social and psychological theories play a significant role in providing further insight about how these females' school experiences affect them physically and emotionally. Interviews and observations provide the necessary foundation to formulate what is beneficial to these students and how, so that their educational experiences may be impacted positively. As a result, Muhajabat Theory evolves along with how the school curriculum, teachers and administrators could collaboratively make the educational system inclusive and welcoming for them.

Research regarding hijab has emerged within the last decade. England, France, Canada and the United States are countries whose governments and citizens are critically involved, both politically and socially, in determining what role hijab plays in their societies. Whether concerned with political decision making or social implications, scholarly writings and debates have left no uncertainty that hijab and its role in European and Western societies cannot be ignored. Research regarding hijab will be elaborated upon in the literature review.

In the Name of Allah, The Beneficent,
The Merciful

DEDICATION

This work is dedicated to the memory of Safiyyah Rasheedah Abdur-Rahman May 23, 1972—January 27, 2001. Without your love, support, kindness, commitment and encouragement, I would not have attempted to pursue this degree. I love you always.

ACKNOWLEDGEMENTS

First and foremost, I would like to thank the Almighty Creator for giving me this opportunity. I would like to acknowledge all of the people who supported my efforts and encouraged me to pursue my goals. I must give special thanks to my parents, grandparents and my husband for their love and support.

I want to thank Professor Lubna Chaudhry for her profound support. Thank you to Professor Holly Hansen-Thomas and Professor Gladys Jimenez-Munoz. Special thanks to Professor Judy Kugelmass. You will never know how much I appreciate you supporting me in this endeavor.

CHAPTER I

INTRODUCTION

My first name is Jawairriya (pronounced Jew-air-re-yah). I am an American whose chosen way of life is the practice of Islam. Islam is a religion and way of life, and a person who ascribes to its tenets is a Muslim. "Muslim" can be defined as a person who submits to and accepts the will of God. I was born and raised as a Muslim by parents who were raised Christian and converted to the Muslim faith in the 1960's. Growing up, I enjoyed a healthy family life with my parents and siblings as well as grandparents, aunts, uncles, and cousins of varied religious backgrounds that include Baptist, Presbyterian and African Methodist. I have a diverse and rich family heritage. My family consists of African and Native Americans who were and are professional nurses, teachers, social workers, lawyers and businessmen.

I am a *muhajaba* (singular form of muhajabat). This means that I wear *hijab* (Muslim head scarf) whenever I leave my home. According to the teachings of Islam (Madani, 1995), once a female reaches the age of puberty, she should wear a hijab. A hijab is a head covering that usually covers the hair, neck, and a portion of the chest. For the purpose of this book, this is the definition that will be used. However, there are multiple beliefs and interpretations by Muslims who have various opinions regarding how Muslim females are supposed to cover their bodies. Usually the hijab is worn when venturing outside of the home and in the presence of men who are not immediate relatives such as one's father, grandfathers, brothers, or sons. I have worn hijab throughout my educational career and my experiences surrounding this fact have had a profound impact on my social and educational experiences.

My educational experiences have been as dynamic as my heritage. I perceive my educational background as being unique in the United States. Throughout my elementary and secondary years, I attended a private Muslim school. My first experience as a student in public education began in community college. Being the only muhajaba in my college classes had a profound effect on my growth and development. I had been unaware of the fact that there were many people who knew absolutely nothing about Islam and its teachings. It was only when I began community college in the fall of 1990 that I became aware of how my presence caused certain inquisitiveness among my classmates. I began to comprehend that this was due to my wearing hijab and being recognizably Muslim. I arrived at this conclusion after overhearing comments made by individuals on campus referring to my hijab.

The questions consistently asked by fellow students and professors pertained to my wearing hijab. Once I transferred to a four-year institution, this did not change. I remember sitting in classrooms where students would talk in low tones and attempt to whisper to one another about my hijab. I would always do my best to ignore this type of behavior, and I was always happy when my classes were over and I could leave to go to more comfortable and familiar surroundings. As a result, wearing hijab has had a considerable effect on how I view the public educational experience.

The negative experiences I had as a college student caused me to reflect upon how the hijab is perceived by others, whether positively or negatively. I can remember when I was a freshman at community college and waiting in line at the college bookstore. Two female students standing behind me began talking to one another about my hijab. They made several references to how stupid and weird it must be to walk around with one's hair covered all the time. They were not even slightly perturbed when I turned around and made eye contact with them, nor did they seem to care about the obvious glares I was sending in their direction. Pondering such memories made me realize that younger students in public high schools could have experienced or are experiencing some of the same things that I experienced as an adult college student.

As the number of Muslims continues to grow in the United States from the approximate 6 million Muslims in 2005, (Ulen, 2005, p. 42), so too does the number of Muslim students in attendance at public schools. I believe my research about the educational and social experiences of muhajabat attending public schools can provide a greater understanding of Muslim females in education and may also prove to be the beginning of a powerful dialogue that will improve Muslim and non-Muslim educational and social relations. This study may serve as a vehicle for understanding, explaining and clarifying such things as the desire of many Muslim females to obey what they believe is God's commandment of modesty, while removing the negative images (e.g. that Muslim women are abused and oppressed) applied to so many of us by non-Muslims. Gaining an understanding about hijab and Muslim females requires an understanding of Islam as a way of life. This may help non-Muslims to relate to those who view humility towards the Creator, and devotion to Him as directly linked to their dress (hijab) and actions. In order to conceive how intricate the subject of hijab is, it is important to learn about the various reasons some Muslim females' veil.

Hijab can have multiple meanings. The hijab worn by Muslim women may mean that they are aware of the Muslim teachings and they are attempting to follow them, or it may have a deeper and more personal meaning. My understanding of hijab is that it is a badge of honor and when worn by females who are Muslim connotes modesty, dignity and obedience to the Almighty by adhering to Holy Qur'an. Wearing hijab brings me closer to God and serves as a constant reminder that He is ever present and watchful over all that I do. I believe that God enjoins modesty and I am one of many Muslims who desire to obey His commandments.

This reality has not been widely accepted by non-Muslims in the United States. Muslim women who wear hijab here are often portrayed in the media as abused and controlled. "In popular Western media, such as movies and television, Muslim women are depicted as passive victims of masculine dominance, either fully shrouded and demeaned or semi-naked and kept in harems for the fulfillment of male sexual fantasies" (Haddad, Smith & Moore, 2006, p. 22). This is not an accurate description of American Muslim females. The belief that Muslim females observe hijab because men force them to do so insults some Muslim females who have based their decision on their understanding of Islam. It is not simply a case of Muslim males abusing and neglecting Muslim females. With respect to this belief, Shaikh (2003) says, "The realities of gender dynamics in Islam are as complex and polymorphous as the realities of women in other religious, social, and political contexts" (p. 148). Understanding this may enable those who are unfamiliar with Islam and Muslims to have an open mind when dealing with muhajabat. Hopefully it will bring to light the need for non-Muslims to look at the experience of the muhajabat from a Muslim versus non-Muslim perspective. Shaikh (2003) writes,

> Those Western feminist discourses that represent the hijab as simply symbolic of Muslim women's subjugation miss both the particularity of such a phenomenon as well as the multiple levels of meanings that it may have for different Muslim women. (p. 152)

These types of discourse do not differentiate between muhajabat living in countries with geographic, political and religious variations which require contextually focusing on their experiences. In addition, the individuality of muhajabat is negated, but it is their individuality that will provide their reasons for veiling. It is my desire to move the discourse on muhajabat away from the belief that Muslim females who wear hijab are being subjugated by men, and towards an approach where the muhajabat are allowed to provide others with an understanding of their experience in their own words.

This project is different from other muhajabat studies for two reasons: 1) It is specific to the muhajabat experiences of adolescents attending public school and seeks to not only share their experiences but also develop solutions to some of the problems they face in their educational and social environments; 2) Feminist theory is not used as the framework for explaining or understanding the muhajabat experience in the same way that it grounds other muhajabat literature. Literature about the muhajabat experience such as Bullock's (2002) *Rethinking Muslim Women and the Veil* includes discussing the veil from multiple approaches. For example, feminism, terminology, interviews, perceptions and other numerous themes are covered. However, there are no chapters dedicated to possible solutions or improvements in the lives of the females these texts are about. This text seeks to not only share muhajabat experience but to create and develop answers.

In addition, there are three themes that are missing or insufficient in the muhajabat literature reviewed:

1. A comprehensive and detailed explanation of hijab from the Muslim perspective.
2. Grounding muhajabat discourse in theory other than, or in addition to, feminism.
3. The importance of social identity and stigma as it relates to the muhajabat experience.

The following alphabetic annotations will further explain the themes missing or insufficient with current hijab literature. a. A detailed explanation of why some Muslim females wear hijab, and the Muslim teachings that compel them to do so is not found in the current literature pertaining to muhajabat. I believe that it is necessary to provide a comprehensive and inclusive study of hijab in order for it to be correctly understood. What the Qur'an, Hadith and Shariah impart regarding hijab is relevant and significant to the muhajabat experience. Therefore, I found it to be an essential component of my research that could not be avoided.

The purpose of providing the Qur'an's injunctions regarding hijab in this research is to demonstrate that they are presented in the Muslim holy book. It is a symbol of the Muslim faith and directly links modesty and faith as a constituent of a Muslim's way of life. Learning what the Sunnah or teachings of the Prophet Muhammad (peace be upon him) counsel in relation to hijab provides a practical perspective of the Qur'an's injunctions and yields what aspirations a muhajaba may try to achieve as a veiled Muslim female. The Shariah (Islam's law) supports the teachings of the Qur'an and Sunnah. Before examining the effects on students of wearing hijab in public schools, we must determine the religious reasons for veiling. b. There is no one group or category in which feminists can be placed. There is a group of feminists that some may label 'liberals' (Bullock 2002) who attempt to use categories unaffiliated with the mainstream to examine muhajabat issues. Nonetheless, the tendency by feminists to equate veiling with oppression creates concern as to whether or not the muhajabat experience can be fairly and accurately portrayed without a colonial, oriental, missionary and Western slant.

Feminist theory is the underpinning for much of the literature addressing the muhajaba plight (Bullock, 2002; Haw, 1998 & Zine, 2006). It is used primarily to explore and point out the connections between gender and social resistance in the context of public education. These writings are dominated by the questioning of assumptions and discussions of globalization and political ideologies. I chose not to use feminist theory as the underlying support of my research after reading literature by feminists (Jasser, 1999 & Mernissi, 1997) that implied that the hijab is a symbol of subordination for Muslim females. c. How muhajabat view themselves and are perceived by others is integral to my understanding of the muhajabat experience. The rituals of interaction explained by Goffman (1967) include individuals sharing a common mood that shapes behavior. The social and school interactions of muhajabat produce attitudes among them that emerge from negative emotional experiences. When this occurs, individuals gravitate towards others for support and in the case of muhajabat, it is usually their peers with whom they can express and share their feelings pertaining to their school experiences.

Symbolic interaction is the theory Goffman (1969) developed that expressed how human interaction and the conscious and unconscious mind specified ways in which symbols and actions results. The practicality of surviving and being successful in one's surroundings (public schools) is a supporting factor of this theory. This theory can be used to address how people feel about muhajabat and how muhajabat feel about the people with whom they interact; how muhajabat observe others and are observed by others; how muhajabat describe others and are described by others. Analyzing these essential social components is necessary for learning about and understanding what social occurrences take place in their educational environment.

Public School Students and Hijab

This study demonstrates how some students wearing hijab while attending public schools are faced with complex social issues. As muhajabat students struggle to become members of their school environments, they experienced a culmination of emotions such as low self-esteem, alienation, stigma, pride and self-valuing. In addition, they also endured stereotyping and prejudice. The description of events by the muhajabat whom this research is focused upon challenged the public school environment to acknowledge and accept their differences. Each participant valued their education and are consistent in their pursuit to become successful high school graduates. Although their school experiences have been both positive and negative, their identity as muhajabat remains constant and their desire to assimilate into public school culture is integral to their existence.

Numerous writings about hijab argue against one-dimensional views of this practice. Nevertheless, they vary regarding how veiling should be addressed socially. Alvi, Hoodfar and McDonough (2003) suggest a framework in which the veil is situated within clothing's history and is used to invoke political and social action. Bullock (2002) analyzes various methodologies of why Muslim women veil and challenges many of the assumptions made by the general populous. In contrast, Haddad, Smith and Moore (2006) describe hijab as being "Among the most visible ways a woman can affirm her identity with Islam". (p. 9) They cite Muslim identity as a driving force behind the current veiling phenomena.

I believe it is important to create a new paradigm attentive to muhajabat, one that specifically focuses on adolescents negotiating space for themselves in American public schools. Thus far, much of the literature regarding hijab and the United States focuses on women functioning within the larger society. My interests pertain to the public educational system and the muhajabat students it serves. The exploration of this research topic, *Veiled Voices: Muhajabat in Public Schools,* evolved out of this interest.

Originally, this muhajabat research began as a pilot study completed in 2001 at the university I attended. This occurred at a time when I had already experienced some of hijab's social effects. I decided to survey muhajabat on the university campus about their classroom and school experiences. My interest was further piqued after discovering that several of the students shared frustrations regarding teacher attitudes and what they construed as negative experiences. As an educator working with elementary and high school students, I marveled at the thought of high school muhajabat possibly going through some of the same struggles and decided to pursue this topic.

This issue has become increasingly relevant in today's world. Muslim dress and hijab were thrust to the forefront of public scrutiny in the United States after the 1991 Gulf War and subsequently after September 11, 2001 (Haddad, Smith & Moore, 2006). As a result, hijab has been a consistent topic of conversation in the media, political arena and the general public. Schools are not exempt from this. Challenging incidents in our country involving hijab, such as an Alabama motor vehicle department prohibiting the wearing of hijab in driver's license photographs a nursing student at Fairleigh Dickinson University in New Jersey being told she could not wear her head covering, or a Des Moines convenient store refusing to employ a Muslim woman unless she agreed not to cover her head (see appendices D, E, F), have contributed to the deterioration of the fibers that binds our society together. Academic institutions are filled with people representing the diversity within our common culture and none are exempt from society's state of affairs. Few Americans have a genuine understanding of Islam's teachings regarding hijab. For some muhajabat, Muslim teachings and understandings are the important key as to why they veil. This book seeks to provide insight into who muhajaba are in the context of their religious way of life and how this connects with being educated in a public environment. The pertinent questions posed are:

1. What are the educational and social effects of muhajabat receiving a public education?
2. What are the necessary educational and social components needed for muhajabat to be successful (ie. experience feelings of well-being) in public schools?

Arguments surrounding hijab and schools have galvanized in multiple countries including the United States of America. Zine (2006) articulated the debate about the banning of hijab in Quebec and French public schools. She discussed the widespread notion that hijab is oppressive to females and challenged this idea by pointing out that "Stereotypes deny the agency of Muslim women who wear the veil, and reduces the multiple meanings associated with the veil to a single negative referent". (p. 241) Stereotyping and its ill effects in relation to muhajabat may be reduced when:

- An understanding of hijab's origins is known;
- Accepting muhajaba as individuals that are part of a larger group occurs;
- There is increased knowledge about why some Muslims veil.

Inquiry into the ways in which muhajabat embrace or contest their educational and social experiences will assist in answering the above research questions.

This research will bring forth information and insight regarding the educational and social experiences of three North American muhajabat public school students residing in New York and three in North Carolina. This task was not a simple one. A combination of the muhajabat discourses, interviews of Muslim females and analytic inquiry are all components of this research. In this research, I am not going to generalize the muhajabat experience and include Muslim females throughout the world although there may be commonalities with international muhajabat experiences. The historical, theological, ideological and cultural understanding of hijab varies with age, experience and religious knowledge. For older muhajabat who grasp the social and political implications of being a muhajabat in the West, the hijab may be viewed as a symbol of resistance. Nevertheless, there are adolescent muhajabat that never make this connection because it is not applicable to their understanding as teenagers. These adolescent muhajabat are the ones I will depict by using photographic representations along with interviews, surveys and observations.

Choosing Hijab

It is necessary to explain that there are women who clearly identify themselves as Muslim, but do not believe that wearing a hijab is a requirement of Islam's faith. Hijab has become a controversial topic even amongst Muslims. There are Muslim women who state that they choose not to wear the hijab, although the Qur'an contains references to its observance. Dr. Mernissi is a native Moroccan who describes herself as a feminist Muslim. She is a renowned sociologist and has authored several books relating to Muslim females and their social status. Muslim females and hijab have been one of the many topics she studied. She defines hijab as having three dimensions:

The concept of the word hijab is three-dimensional, and the three dimensions often blend into one another. The first dimension is a visual one: to hide something from sight. The root of the verb hijaba means, 'to hide.' The second dimension is spatial: to separate, to mark a border, to establish a threshold. And finally, the third dimension is ethical: it belongs to the realm of the forbidden. So we have not just tangible categories that exist in the reality of the senses—the visual, the spatial— but also an abstract reality in the realm of ideas. A space hidden by a hijab is a forbidden space. (Mernissi, 1987, p. 93)

To Mernissi, hijab as mentioned in Holy Qur'an refers to a form of separation and not to a physical covering. In fact, she believes that the references to hijab in Holy Qur'an are negative and that men expound on this negativity. She states that:

It is strange indeed to observe the modern course of this concept, which from the beginning had a strongly negative connotation in the Koran. The very sign of the person who is damned, excluded from the privileges and spiritual grace to which the Muslim has access, is claimed in our day as a symbol of Muslim identity, manna for the Muslim woman. (Mernissi, 1987, p. 97)

I respect Dr. Mernissi's opinion, but I have to disagree with her interpretation. I have been unable to find in the Holy Qur'an the negative connotation she is referring to and she does not specifically provide in her research a written record of what she is referencing. I also believe such writings have a severe negative impact on Muslim females and their right to wear hijab. When interpretation of religious requirements are provided by a person who professes to be Muslim and it agrees with what is socially or politically correct within the general public, such interpretation is consistently referenced by non-Muslims and used to promote various political agendas.

However, there are other renowned feminists such as Minh-ha (1988) who acknowledge and respect difference and utilize it to provide and promote an understanding of identity. With regard to veiling, Min-ha states:

> If the act of unveiling has a liberating potential, so does the
> act of veiling. It all depends on the context in which such
> an act is carried out, or more precisely, on how and where
> women see dominance. Difference should neither be defined
> by the dominant sex nor by the dominant culture. (p. 372)

In contrast to Mernissi, Min-ha does not attempt to interpret why veiling is good or evil; rather, she focuses on the reality of veiling as it relates to the individual in her quest to resist repression and dominance and defiantly stands up for acceptance of difference.

The anti-hijab movement and anti-hijab decision making has become a public concern here in the United States. An example of this is what occurred in January of 2004 in the state of Alabama. This controversy was argued about publicly on many of the national cable news channels. Alabama refused to allow Muslim women to obtain or renew their driver licenses without removing their hijab. This decision sparked national opposition and was added to the list of anti-Islam/anti-Muslim actions increasingly prevalent in the United States, as well as many other countries throughout the world. These types of incidents are occurring more frequently. Haddad, Smith & Moore (2006) found that "Many hundreds of incidents have been recorded over the past four years of Muslim women being subjected to offensive and even physically harmful abuse by those who find their Muslim dress objectionable or think that wearing such clothing somehow identifies them as being terrorist". (p. 15)

I found it interesting to discover that the Alabama Department of Public Safety's policy banning head coverings in driver license photographs was challenged after several Muslim women from that state complained to the Council on American-Muslim Relations (CAIR), after being prevented from renewing or obtaining licenses. Rizwan Qureshi, a CAIR Civil Rights Coordinator stated that "Alabama's existing policy actually hinders proper identification by law enforcement authorities in the field because the Muslim women drivers would appear one way in the license photographs and look quite different in person". (www.cair-net) This issue would not have been so swiftly resolved had not Muslim leaders and individuals in Birmingham and Montgomery, along with the American Civil Liberties Union, immediately met with state officials. This is a flagrant example of institutionalized discrimination against Muslim females who wear hijab.

Females wearing hijab and being identifiably Muslim are now matters of international concern. France and Singapore have banned the wearing of the hijab in public educational institutions. Turkey, whose population is predominately Muslim, continues to arrest and detain muhajabat who attempt to enter schools or government buildings. Belgium and Germany are currently discussing imposing similar bans. It has become quite clear that wearing a hijab is becoming very risky in some countries, including the United States (Haddad, Smith & Moore, 2006).

Muslim Women, Hijab and Identity

The first wife of the Prophet, Khadijah [alternate spelling Khodayjah] was most probably the first female convert to Islam and muhajaba who clearly possessed multiple identities (i.e. Arab woman, wife, mother, businesswoman, etc.). Khadijah was a shrewd and successful businesswoman. In addition, she was an honored wife and mother who balanced both business and home life: "As well as being a wife, Khadijah was also a friend to her husband, the sharer of his inclinations and ideals to a remarkable degree" (Lings, 1983, p. 37). Khadijah was said to have been morally good and the epitome of Muslim wifely perfection:

> The virtues and good qualities of Khodayjah (May Allah Be Pleased With Her) were numerous, her perfections and accomplishments innumerable. She was the first who believed in the prophetship of the prince of the righteous. (Jilani, 1983, p. 763)

[1]When speaking about the Holy Last Messenger Muhammad (Peace Be Upon Him), PBUH is used after his name to connote respect. This same practice is used when speaking about the women of his household (May Allah Be Pleased With Them) and other honored women for the first time.

Her righteousness and dedication to Islam allowed her to accomplish great things. As a matter of fact, it is mentioned in Holy Qur'an that Khadijah is one of the four honored women. These ladies have been granted the most blessed stations in paradise. They are Asiya the wife of Pharoah; Maryam mother of Jesus; Fatima, daughter of Prophet Muhammad; and Khadijah.

Khadijah is both a pious and successful example of a muhajabat and provides Muslim females of today with an opportunity to reflect upon previous struggles that can help guide them through life. Debates about Muslim identity are emerging constantly because of global events related to the Muslim world. One example of looking closely at Muslim and Muslim women's identity issues is Khan's book entitled *Muslim Women Crafting a North American Identity.*

> Talk of identity predictably provokes intense reactions and emotions. Many persons who consider questions of identity inescapable are equal in intensity to those who are weary of identity discourse. (Headley, 2002, p. 45)

Throughout history, people with minority status have had to explain or rationalize their identity to the dominant group; for example, Native and African Americans in the United States:

> Dominant groups, by definition, set the parameters within which the subordinates operate. The dominant group holds the power and authority in society relative to the subordinates and determines how that power and authority may be acceptably used. (Tatum, 1997, p. 23)

In reference to Muslim females, wearing hijab does not seem to be acceptable to the dominant group. The unacceptability of hijab has resulted in Muslim females having to defend their right to wear it. Many Muslims are also struggling to help non-Muslims understand that hijab is more than a cloth covering for the head (Ali 2005, Bullock 2002, Zine 2006). Observing hijab means dressing modestly and covering oneself, but it also means practicing modesty in speech, walking, sitting, and in general conduct. For this reason hijab is a component of identity because it represents an attitude, a behavior, a belonging to the group of chaste, dignified, modest females.

I believe this way of discussing hijab is done to move the conversation away from Islam. Framing or citing hijab as an identity issue is less controversial. It should be understood that those Muslim females who do not wear hijab choose not to do so. There may be multiple reasons for this decision. One reason for this is that living in a democratic, Judeo-Christian society can become increasingly difficult when one is a practicing Muslim. This happens because of the following issues:

1. Islam is a way of life encompassing all of life's facets and does not separate mosque from state. Freedom comes from worshipping the Creator and practicing His will as the Qur'an (Holy book sacred to Muslims), Hadith (record of the Prophet's practices) and Shari'ah (Muslim law) teach. This is in strong contrast to the Western philosophy of separating church and state, encouraging the notion that religion is for the home and thus hijab is also.

2. Some women's organizations and many politicians have used the media to spread what I believe is an intentionally incorrect Western perspective on the evils of hijab.

    For example, the evils of burqas and veiling in Afghanistan. This notion was given intense media coverage even after the Taliban were out of power and Afghan women continued with the practice of veiling and wearing their traditional burqas.

3. Persons who refer to themselves as Muslim but who are oft-times cultural Muslims may provide misinformation about hijab requirements. This can be due to a lack of knowledge or understanding of the Qur'anic teachings. I define a cultural Muslim as a person who comes from generations of Muslims or is born and raised in a country where Islam is the dominant religion. The person then assumes Islam as their own religion, but they do not necessarily practice Islam as a way of life, nor have they necessarily studied or learned about Islam. Examples of the misinformation that they provide are: a) 'It is not acceptable in the West so muhajabat should not make life difficult'; b) 'It is a choice. Muhajabat really do not have to wear it'; c) 'Hijab only has to be observed when around Muslims in the mosque, Eid celebration, etc'.

Hijab is a commandment in the Holy Qur'an and supported by Hadith and Shari'ah. These commandments are also challenged and continuously interpreted by Muslims and some non-Muslims alike. The topic of hijab is clear and substantiated in Islam's teachings. Nonetheless, it is also clear that people have choices. In my opinion, each and every human being has a right to choose how he/she will live and/or what beliefs they will have or practice. The point of my synopsis is that a selected choice is not the same as a choice offered by the Creator as part of the Muslim way of life, although such choices exist. This is a very important distinction relevant to hijab that should be recognized in order to effectively understand the muhajabat experience.

There is a good deal of literature that explains and discusses the historical and religious context of veiling and hijab. This information can assist in helping us further our knowledge and understanding, and gauge its applicability to the modern day muhajabat in our society and those attending public schools.

Muslim Subgroups and Identity

Muslim immigrants from over sixty countries have settled in the United States. These groups of immigrants include various nationalities that can be broken into additional subgroups. "For instance, Pakistanis can be divided into at least five linguistic subgroups. Therefore, it is realistic to say that there are over 100 subgroups of Muslims in America". (Ghayur, 1981, p. 154)

With the variety of Muslims in the United States, the binding fibers connecting each group is the affirmation of their belief in One God and recognizing and acknowledging Muhammad as His last and final Messenger. Testifying to this is perhaps the single unifying connector of Muslim peoples descending from various races, tribes and ethnicities. The way these groups interpret and apply the teachings of Islam depends on their culture. Nonetheless, the ideal that Muslims are a single community irrespective of race or ethnicity is still the common belief and goal, even if it has not been achieved thus far in some communities.

Although multiple races, tribes, and ethnicities of Muslims exist, I believe that it is perhaps easier to break Muslims into two distinct groups to assist in defining what Muslim identity is in the United States: 1) The first group of Muslims has chosen Islam as their way of life. This group endeavors to practice the religious tenets in their everyday life functions. 2) The second group comes from a Muslim heritage and acknowledges that there is One Lord (Allah) and that the Prophet Muhammad is His Messenger. This second group does not always practice the tenets of Islam in their everyday life. These differences are significant, and they make it difficult for non-Muslims and Muslims alike to differentiate between faith and practice:

> How then is it possible to distinguish between those Muslims who are culturally or ethnically defined with Islam and those who are motivated by the pillars and the creed of Islam? In contemporary times there is no official control of Muslims' Muslim practices. The individual is responsible for her/his own Muslim performance. (Roald, 2000, p. 22)

This fact makes it virtually impossible to characterize Muslims as a group and to understand and answer the question, 'What is Muslim identity'?

Muslim identity has to do with the beliefs and practices associated with the everyday life of Muslims. It is also what separates Muslims from non-Muslims. There is no one definition of Muslim/American Muslim identity; rather, there are components that contribute to shaping the identity of Muslims:

> Identity formation is a complex process that allows for the intervention of both historical and material forces and human agency. In the specific case of the Muslim community in North America, one can clearly see that both historical forces and political agencies are shaping the emerging identity of American Muslims, the political forces both local and global in nature. (Khan, 2003, p. 175)

It is imperative that issues of religious and cultural identity are given close and careful study when trying to understand the experiences of muhajabat. When discussing identity, Dorinne Kondo, anthropologist and University of Southern California professor, states, "Identities are bounded entities containing some essence or substance that is expressed in distinctive attributes". (Kondo, 1990, p. 33) One's identity changes at any given time. Identity is not always singular, and multiple identities can coexist within individuals. A person's identity may be altered depending on their beliefs, experiences, and so on. "Identities are not only constructed but are constantly produced and reproduced through social practices and identity discourses". (Khan, 2003, p. 176) As muhajabat socialize in their educational environment, the way they are perceived and treated will affect how they perceive themselves. Muhajabat reconstruct their identity throughout their experiences. Therefore, identity constancy cannot be assumed.

Wearing hijab may constitute a small or large part of a female's identity. For instance, after conversing with some African and African-American females who observe hijab, some felt that their racial experiences outweighed their religious experiences. However, hijab is still a part of their identity. Some females who are unable to comfortably define their own identity and freely express who they are may not know how to connect with other muhajabat or females in their minority group. Oft-times wearing the hijab may link together females and women whose individual identities vary greatly. Hekman (1999) found that a person's identity is diverse. She writes, "Our identity is a specific marker of how we define ourselves at any particular moment in life" and it is not a crystallized formation that remains solidified through time. (p. 7) It is altered individually as well as by group dynamics. Some muhajabat may experience identity problems that are different in contrast to other muhajabat at various times in their lives. If a person is unable to discover and be comfortable with who they are they may be unable to associate and connect with others in their group. It is necessary to examine the muhajabat experience within the context of understanding its direct connection to identity. Muhajabat experiences may run from simple to complex and they may be based on the individual's family life and social environment.

Wearing a hijab can be looked at in two distinct ways. It can be considered to be an aspect of both individual identity (why and how an individual chooses to wear hijab) and communal/group identity (why and how the overall community believes the hijab should be worn). Ann Sofie Roald (2000) believes:

> The understanding of identity involves both identity at an
> individual level and identity at a group level. Identity on an
> individual level comprises distinctive characteristics such
> as personality, physical and intellectual traits, and identity

> on a group level comprises social categories such as group-
> belonging, class, nationality and sex. (p. 13)

Individual and group identity both have an effect on muhajabat. In various Muslim communities consisting of muhajabat, group belonging may determine how hijab is worn. Whether or not it is always pinned or wrapped underneath the neck or if fastening or tying it behind the head is acceptable. Although there are some muhajabat who belong to a larger group, they may choose to individually contradict the hijab practices of their larger affiliation and wear a hijab style unique and all their own.

The communal/group aspect of wearing hijab is directly related to one's membership in a Muslim community, including cultural and religious beliefs and practices, Muslim etiquette, group culture, and moral growth and development. Once a girl attains the age of puberty she may begin to observe hijab in public according to teachings of Islam. How hijab should be worn (pinned, tied, thrown over one shoulder, etc.) is sometimes an issue addressed not merely by an individual, but by the group deemed more knowledgeable in determining how the community will be viewed. The relationship between individuals and social norms as described by Erving Goffman (1963) suggests that individuals who share values adhere to similar conduct codes or attributes that are considered normal. Nevertheless, this does not occur all of the time.

As a result, those who do not share these same behaviors or practices are considered peculiar and deviant. Observing hijab may, however, be considered abnormal within the social context of American society. Muslims are not only minorities in the United States, but given the current political climate following 9/11, covering one's hair with a hijab may cause negative attention and may also be perceived as deviant behavior.

Depending on age, family, life experiences, etc. observing hijab may have multiple meanings, which contribute to females having multiple identities. By the time I was in my late teens, my Muslim identity was extremely important to me, and observing hijab became a practice I felt validated me as a Muslim. It also provided me with security as I deemed modesty to be overwhelmingly important. This did not mean that my sisters experienced the same feelings.

This was only how I, as an individual, internalized the hijab. A large part of my identity as a Muslim female became directly connected to wearing the hijab. To comprehend the magnitude of hijab and identity and how they play a role in the context of adolescent Muslim female experience, an understanding of hijab's origins must be learned. Subsequently, the origins of hijab and Islam, Qur'an and the Sunnah demonstrate how entwined hijab and identity are with belief.

Origins of Hijab

Veiling is not limited to any one religion or way of life and predates Islam (Vogelsang—Eastwood, 1996). Historically, veiling was used as a status symbol to separate females considered honorable or decent from females of 'ill repute' (females available for sex). When researching the history of veiling, Vogelsang-Eastwood (1996) discovered that verifiable evidence existed that veiling antedates Islam:

> With respect to veiling, the range of potential information is considerable. There are numerous representations from all over the world, including sculptures, paintings, and relics, which depict veiled figures. There are written accounts including lists of dowries and receipts for objects, which record the presence and use of veils. There are also laws dating back to the second millennium BC in Mesopotamia, which forbid certain groups of women to go out of their houses without being veiled. (1996, p. 15)

Islam did not begin the practice of women veiling in public. The historical accounts of this practice become relevant when placed in the context of the current hijab debate, which places blame upon Muslims for initiating and enforcing an 'evil' trend. It is important to know that prior to the advent of Islam veiling gave an immediate indication as to part of a female's identity. She was looked upon as a female under male protection if veiled or as available for male gratification if not veiled.

"In the East women have always lived in seclusion, not appearing in public unless closely veiled, not seeing the men who visit their husbands and brothers, nor even taking their meals with the men of their own family". (Nevin, 1875, p. 101) This does not mean that veiling was limited to the Middle East. As a matter of fact, many of the paintings and sculptures of veiled women were procured in Europe. Therefore, it can be assumed that veiling was a practice for women from societies that were culturally and religiously different but that agreed upon veiling as an important value.

Understanding some of the historical roots of veiling can give some insight into the Muslim female's use of hijab, but it does not provide Islam's explanation. Before embarking on Islam's teachings of hijab, a brief description of what hijab means is necessary. The word 'hijab' is an Arabic word used to describe various forms of veiling by Muslim females throughout the world. "Hidjab [sic] is used as any veil placed in front of a person or an object in order to conceal it from view or to isolate it" (Donzel, 1971, p. 359). I give this definitive definition because the word "hijab" as it is used today is not a precise translation from the Arabic word.

> Hijab is derived from the root h-j-b; its verbal form hajaba translates as "to veil, to seclude, to screen, to conceal, to form a separation, to mask." Hijab translates as "cover, wrap, curtain, veil, screen, partition. The European term "veil" (with its correlate "seclusion"), therefore, fails to capture these nuances, and oversimplifies a complex phenomenon. (El-Guindi, 1999, p. 157)

The word hijab has been equated with veiling primarily due to translation. Although it is used to represent a visual image of hijab, veiling does not describe its meaning and purpose.

Islam, Qur'an and Hijab

A Muslim is one who submits to the will of Allah (Lord) by following the Holy Qur'an and the teachings of the Prophet Muhammad (Peace Be Upon Him). Islam is the way of life for Muslims. It is considered a way of life because every possible aspect of a Muslim's being can be guided by following Holy Qur'an and Hadith (compilation of the Prophet's teachings). Solutions to life's problems, as well as direction in social interaction, economics, education and parenting are provided. In the life of every Muslim, Islam does not separate the religious from the public (Hanifi, 1980).

Islam's faith is based on five pillars. They are: 1) *Kalimah* or testifying that there is one God and that Muhammad is the true prophet of God; 2) *Salat,* or prayer; 3) *Saum,* or fasting; 4) *Zakat,* or tax; and 5) *Hajj,* or pilgrimage. The five pillars of Islam encompass the basic practices that every Muslim, regardless of denomination, must follow.

(1) Iman, or faith, consists of the belief in one Lord (Allah), His books (Qur'an, Torah, etc.), His angels (Gabriel, Michael, etc.), His prophets (Muhammad, Jesus, Moses, etc.) and the Day of Resurrection.

(2) Prayer is offered five times a day: 1) *Fajr,* or morning prayer; 2) *Zuhr,* or noon Prayer; 3) *Asr,* or late afternoon prayer; 4) *Maghrib,* or sunset prayer; and 5) *Isha,* or night prayer.

(3) Fasting is the third pillar of Islam's faith. It is obligatory during the month of Ramadan upon every healthy Muslim male and female. While fasting, Muslims must abstain from food, drink, and sexual relations from pre-dawn till sunset. Females who are pregnant, breast-feeding or menstruating are not required to fast.

(4) Zakat, or tax, is a requirement for all Muslims. Its purpose is to help those less fortunate than oneself, the poor, widows and orphans: "It tends to counteract the trend towards the accumulation and concentration of wealth and to reduce the gulf between the rich and the poor". (Hanifi, 1980, 98)

(5) Hajj (pilgrimage) is incumbent upon every Muslim who is in good health and can afford the expense. Hajj consists of a journey to Mecca and its environs and includes circumambulation of the Ka'ba (Prayer house built by Prophet Abraham). In order to begin understanding Islam, it is necessary to learn about the pillars of this faith. Continuing this learning requires understanding about the Prophet Muhammad (peace be upon him).

The Prophet Muhammad (PBUH) was born in Mecca more than 1400 years ago (Jilani, 1983). He was the son of Abdullah and Amina. The Holy Qur'an was revealed to the Prophet on the 27th night of Ramadan when he was contemplating. Muslims believe that the first revelation to the Prophet Muhammad (PBUH) came during his contemplation at Mount Hira. "The essence of the message was, 'There is one God and one humanity' ". (Rahman, 1996, p. 12) Muslims believe that the Qur'an is the word of the one God (Allah), revealed through the Angel Gabriel to the Prophet Muhammad (PBUH). The Holy Qur'an was revealed in the Arabic language and is divided into 114 chapters called *surahs.*

Surah Al-Ahzab in the Holy Qur'an contains the first reference to hijab. "And when ye ask of (the Prophet's wives) what ye may have occasion for, ask it of them from behind a curtain" (Tariq, 1966, p. 361). This particular ayat (verse) was speaking about invitations for meals, guest conduct, and also the etiquette of socialization with women. Many Muslim scholars have explained or interpreted this verse. One explanation given by Ibn Kathir states that:

> Muslims were forbidden from entering the houses of the Prophet as they used to enter each other's houses without permission in the days before Islam. Allah chose modesty and honor for this Ummah and commanded them to observe Hijab. Undoubtedly, this commandment is in respect and honor of this Ummah. (Madani, 1995, p. 4)

The above ayat is not the only one that refers to Muslim females being covered. Allah also commands in ayat 59 of Surah Al-Ahzab:

> O Prophet! Speak to thy wives, and thy daughters, and the wives of the true Believers, that they cast their outer garments (jalabib) over them (when they walk abroad); this (will be) more proper, that they may be known (to be gentle and honorable women) and may not be affronted (by vulgar speech or behavior).
>
> Allah is Forgiving and Merciful. (Translation by Maulana Abdur-Rahman Tariq, 1966, p. 362)

The objective of hijab was to prevent familiarity between males and females who were not related to one another, and to afford females protection from the evils of some men.

Understanding hijab based on the Qur'an's explanation should be done while also looking at injunctions placed on men. The Qur'an does not discriminate against one sex at the expense of another. It should be understood that the previously stated ayats were selected and used based on their content. This in no way negates the fact that throughout the Qur'an, the required etiquette for both men and women is clearly stated. Surah Al-Nur (The Light), ayats 30-31 state:

> O Prophet! Say to the believing men that they should restrain their eyes, and guard their private parts (against adultery); this is purer for them, for Allah is well acquainted with what they do. And say to the believing women that they should restrain their eyes, and preserve their chastity, and display not their decorations, except what (necessarily) appears thereof; and let them draw their head coverings over their bosoms, and not display their decorations except to their husbands or their fathers, or their husbands' fathers, or their sons, or their husbands' sons, or their women, or the (captives) which their right hands possess; or such male attendants as have no need (of women), or young children who have no knowledge of the nakedness of women. And let them not strike their feet, so that what they hide of their ornaments may thereby be known and turn to Allah (for guidance), all together believers, that you may be successful. (Tariq, 1966, p. 293)

These ayats are clear for both men and women and require

1. Lowering one's gaze from looking at what is forbidden;
2. Guarding one's modesty to prevent sexual excitement in others;
3. Concealing one's beauty in front of men, if marriage with them is not forbidden. (Examples of men who are exempted from this rule are fathers, brothers, husbands, sons, and uncles).

Although hijab is a concern for Muslim women, the overall principle of modesty is incumbent upon both men and women. Furthermore, the aim of hijab with its restrictions, prohibitions and exhortations is the preservation and the development of the morality and spirituality of mankind. Both men and women are responsible for working to ensure the achievement of these aims. This responsibility reflects no distinction between men and women. An example of this can be found in the Holy Qur'an. In Surah Al-Ahzab, ayat 35, states:

For Muslim men and women, for believing men and women, for devout men and women, for true men and women, for men and women who are patient and constant, for men and women who humble themselves; for men and women who give in charity, for men and women who fast, for men and women who guard their chastity, and for men and women who engage much in God's praise, for them has God prepared forgiveness and great reward (Tariq, 1966, p. 294).

There are additional ayats in the Holy Qur'an that refer to hijab. I have, however, only selected the ones I believe express the Qur'anic perspectives about hijab that provide the reader with basic information. The Sunnah (teachings of the Prophet Muhammad PBUH) pertaining to hijab can now be addressed.

The Sunnah (The Way in Which the Prophet PBUH lived) & Hijab

A person cannot begin to understand Islam unless he or she learns about the role both Qur'an and Hadith play in the Muslim context: "The word 'Hadith' literally means 'sayings' of the Prophet and Sunnah indicates the practice. Hadith is the narration and record of the Sunnah, and also contains, in addition, some prophetical and historical elements". (Hanifi 1980, p. 15) The Sunnah encompasses all aspects of life including marriage, childbirth and upbringing, eating, sleeping, etc. Many non-Muslims are unaware of the powerful role of the Sunnah in Islam. A person cannot be a Muslim unless he or she accepts that Muhammad is the messenger of the one Creator (Allah) and understand that his life was and is the example for all Muslims to follow. Henceforth, the Qur'an and the Sunnah form an inseparable marriage, which enables both to be jointly used as a guide to its followers in their everyday lives.

The combination of the Qur'an and Sunnah provides an understanding and explanation of the existence of the Lord (Allah), the purpose of humanity, what laws and practices should be followed, and finally, how they should be followed. The Qur'an and Sunnah encompass all of this. Those Muslims who choose to separate the two fail to realize that the very life of the Prophet Muhammad was the practical application of the injunctions of Holy Qur'an. Holy Qur'an is considered a manual for life, and from the example of the Prophet Muhammad we understand how to follow this manual. A prime example can be seen in noticing that there is no mention in Holy Qur'an how the five prescribed prayers should be observed. Nonetheless, there are many commands to offer the five prayers. It is the Prophet Muhammad who taught us the manner that salaat should be performed through his Sunnah. Holy Qur'an can be considered the guide and the Sunnah the practical application in everyday life.

The teachings as regards modesty and hijab are evident in Holy Qur'an. The Hadith then provides specific examples of how modesty and hijab are observed. The teachings of the Prophet are quite clear. Modesty is part of faith. During the Prophet's lifetime, he and the members of his family practiced modesty with the opposite sex, in etiquette as well as dress. All references to the females of his household describe them as modest ladies who observed hijab and wore loose clothing.

The Sunnah pertaining to modesty was not relegated to simply covering a person's head, but rather it focused on the presentation of the entire person. The following are Hadiths in reference to this subject:

> Abu Huraira reported God's Messenger (blessings and peace of Allah be upon him) as saying: Modesty is part of faith and faith is in paradise, but obscenity is a part of hardness of heart and hardness of heart is in hell. It was related by Ahmad & Tirmidhi. (Robson, 1964, p. 1054)

> Aisha reported, Asma, Daughter of Abu Bakr, came to the Messenger of Allah, peace and blessings of Allah be on him and she was wearing thin clothes. The Messenger of Allah, peace and belessings of Allah be on him, turned away his face from her and said: O Asma! When the woman attains her majority, it is not proper that any part of her body should be seen except this and this. And he pointed to his face and his hands. It was related by Abu Dawud. (Ali, 1993, p. 392)

> Narrated Abu Said Al-Khudri: Allah's Messenger forbade two ways of wearing clothes. The two ways were to cover one

shoulder with a garment and leave the other bare; and the other way was to wrap oneself with a garment while sitting in such a way that nothing of that garment would cover one's private parts. (Khan, 1997, p. 390)

Aishah said: May Allah have mercy on the early immigrant women. When the verse (from Holy Qur'an) 'That they should draw their veils over their bosoms' was revealed, they tore their thick outer garments and made veils from them. It was related by Abu Dawud. (Hasan, 1990, p. 1144)

Yahya related to me from Malik from Muslim ibn Abi Maryam from Abu Salih that Abu Hurayra said, 'Women who are naked even though they are wearing clothes, go astray and make others go astray, and they will not enter the Garden and they will not find its scent, and its scent is experienced from as far as the distance traveled in five hundred years'. (Abdarahman, 1982, p. 444)

These are just five hadiths regarding modesty and dress that provide examples of the Prophet's teachings. Guarding one's modesty and preserving honor are both aspects of observing hijab that are incumbent upon every Muslim, male and female alike. There is a hadith that states, "No one has a better sense of honor than Allah, which is why he has forbidden lewdness". (Madani, 1995, p. 51) This hadith clarifies the importance of modesty as ordained by the Creator, while not limiting it to females only.

What is most important regarding the Sunnah and hijab is that it supports the injunctions of modesty and honor as prescribed in the Holy Qur'an. The Prophet Muhammad's references to modesty, hijab, and female attire were always given as a reminder of the Lord's expectations for mankind and achieving solace in the next life. Because this solace is dependent on the deeds and actions accrued in this life, it is of grave importance that the Sunnah regarding hijab and modesty are understood and practiced. In addition to the Qur'an and Sunnah, there is also Shari'ah.

Shari'ah and Hijab

Shari'ah is an Arabic word, which is translated as the 'law of Islam'. This legal perspective encompasses all aspects of a Muslim's life including crime and punishment. "The term 'Shari'at' literally means "the clear path to be followed", but technically it means 'the Law of Islam'. The Shari'ah, as an infallible doctrine of duties, comprises the whole of religious, social, political, domestic and private life of those who profess Islam". (Hanifi, 1980, p. 29)

"The shari'ah is the fundamental and comprehensive law undergirding the divine creation. It will always accompany and guide people on earth, and as such it is a central element of Islam, unifying all believers, and helping them to direct their existence to Allah everyday anew". (Weiss, 2000, p. 41) It is important to note that Shari'ah law can only be enforced in countries that are governed by Muslims. Muslims living in non-Muslim countries cannot be governed by Shari'ah law.

Scholars of Islam compiled a system of rules for several hundred years after the death of the Prophet (PBUH). This compilation is based on Qur'an and Hadith and its purpose is to provide answers to any questions arising in life or to solve any problems that may occur. Four legal schools were founded by the 11th century and are currently still in existence. All Muslims should follow one of the four schools of thought or Islam's law (Hanifi, Shafi, Maliki, and Hanbali). This allows for questions regarding Islam's law to be answered based on the system of rules for a particular school of thought. These schools may differ slightly in interpretation but are nonetheless consistent with their teachings and points of view. However, there are some who call themselves Muslim but choose to follow any or all schools based on their desire to receive answers that are acceptable to their situation at a particular time, rather than committing to one. This behavior results in confusion and contributes to a misinterpretation of the law because there is never a set standard that is being adhered to.

The Shari'ah addresses modes of dress for Muslim men and women. It is required in Shari'ah for men and women to cover their bodies. The private parts for a man encompass the area from his navel to his knees. This portion of a man's body should be covered while in front of others. The private parts for a woman include her entire body except her face and hands. A Muslim woman should never uncover from her chest to her legs even in front of other women.

Prior to Shari'ah injunctions of clothing to promote modesty, dignity, and honor, men and women were taught the importance of lowering the gaze and guarding the eyes against immorality. These are principles found in the Qur'an, Hadith and Shari'ah. Dr. Madani explains that "to create a virtuous society and to protect it from sexual anarchy, the Shari'ah, among other things, has commanded to safeguard the eyes. This is because the eyes serve as a messenger. Not guarding the eyes is the first sign of moral decay". (p. 61) In other words, staring at persons of the opposite gender to elicit attention or to satisfy lustful thoughts is not permissible and should be avoided. Observing hijab and behaving in a modest fashion aids in developing piety. Moreover, the issue of modesty has not been limited to a concern of Muslims, but rather a concern for mankind. Morris (1977) shares that:

> Basically, clothes have three functions: comfort, modesty and display. Comfort is, of course, the utilitarian function of garments, non-social and personal. The second basic function of clothing is that of modesty. In this role, clothing acts as a concealment device. Garments are worn to switch off certain body signals. The 'full frontal' human body can only reduce the sexuality of its approach by hiding the sexual regions in some way (1977, pp. 213-214).

Morris (1977) believes that dressing modestly became necessary as population sizes grew.

> After millions of years living in small tribal units, mankind now moves about in huge urban crowds, surrounded by comparative or total strangers. Under these conditions direct sexual displays have to be tamped down. Body signals have to be switched off. The human body is a mass of gender signals, and every curve of flesh, each bulge and contour, transmits its basic signals to the eyes of interested onlookers. (p. 215)

This is the premise for modesty and hijab found not only in Holy Qur'an and Hadith, but in Shari'ah as well.

In addition to Holy Qur'an, Hadith and Shari'ah, there exists a group of Muslims whose beliefs regarding hijab extends and transcends the purpose and meaning of veiling from the context provided above. These people are called Sufis and are otherwise known as the mystics of Islam's faith.

Sufis and Hijab

O You, my Friend, my ecstasy and aspiration,
Besides You, my heart spurns all other love.
O Beloved, my long-enduring ambition and yearning
Is to behold You.
Among all the pleasures of Paradise
Only union with You do I wish.

Reyhana of Basra (Sufi)   (Nurbakhsh, 1983, p. 117)

People that practice mysticism in Islam are called Sufis. The goal of a Sufi is to become one with the Almighty by purging themselves of worldly desires. Through contemplation, one can attain and achieve various spiritual stages. The love of the Divine illuminates understanding of the purpose of life. The understanding of the spiritual and mystical side of a Sufi is directly related to hijab. There is a Sufi view that, "The whole world is the book of God Most High and that beneath the veil of each atom is hidden the soul-ravishing beauty of the Face of the Beloved". (Smith, 1974, p. 50). Remembrance of God, wakefulness, silence, fasting, and seclusion, are the five basic principles Smith notes that Sufis must practice, to be blessed with unveiling.

For further understanding, I asked a Sheikh of the Qadri Order, His Eminence Syed Mubarik Shah, to define for me what being a Sufi means. The following was his response:

The word Sufi is derived firstly from *soof* (meaning wool) because the Sufia (plural for Sufi) are known to wear woolen or coarse garments depicting their indifference to the luxuries and pleasures of worldly life. Secondly and more essential, Sufi also takes its form from the word *saaf* or pure. From the word saaf, we understand that cleanliness or purity is essential, and the Sufi is the one who adopts the path of purity. This purity is an inner or spiritual purity, the cleanliness of one's intentions, heart, and actions.

The essence of the message of the Sufia is *wahdiyaat* or oneness, i.e. oneness of the Creator, creation, and divine message to mankind through prophets and saints. For the Sufia, mankind in his present state is in a state of forgetfulness. Lifting the veil of forgetfulness, thus attaining the station of *fana* or annihilation is most essential to achieve the goal, which is the Almighty Lord. The peculiarity of the Sufia is that they do not separate humanity on a religious or racial divide, but simply in stations of proximity to the Almighty Creator. They have reached the realization that the Almighty is the Creator of both Moses and Pharaoh, so the ultimate challenge is not a fight of religious differences or beliefs but a waking up by removing our veils of separation from the Creator before being *awakened* by Him on the Last Day.

The hijab is a most essential topic in Sufi terminology because it represents the veiling that inhibits mankind from his goal, i.e. Allah. Removing this hijab is treading the path of being a Sufi. The relationship between the hijab in Sufi terminology and the hijab for ordinary Muslims is that just as Allah is pure and observes hijab from strangers, so too is that there is nothing more sacred between heaven and earth than the purity of a Muslim woman, who by following Allah's example veils herself from strangers and only lifts that veil in the presence of her near and dear ones (husband, father, brothers, etc.). Anything of value must not be displayed for all eyes to see, so Allah veils Himself from all but His lovers, and a Muslim woman veils herself from all but her family. (June 29, 2004).

Sufis believe that hijab is the veil that comes between man and the Almighty due to man's participation in worldly desires: "In the eyes of the mystics, hidjab represents everything that veils the end, all that makes man insensitive to the Divine Reality. The man who is 'veiled' (mahdjub) is he whose heart is closed to the Divine light, because his awareness is dominated by sensual or mental passion". (Donzel, 1971, p. 361)

Although the Sufi perspective on hijab directly relates to an individual and their relationship to becoming annihilated (meaning the worldly self is destroyed so that God is the only focus) into the Creator, one can relate this to the practice of Muslim females wearing hijab. Muslims believe that learning, understanding, and living the will of the Almighty with regard to modesty and hijab requires both women and men to adhere to the will of God. This can be achieved by following the teachings of Qur'an and Hadith. Whether or not hijab is looked at as a mystical separation between man and the Almighty or a headscarf worn by Muslim women, the result is similar. There is physical concealment that should be acknowledged and respected for what it is.

Muslims and Spirituality

The very meaning of the word Muslim (One who submits to the will of God) connotes spiritual acceptance (Shah, 1970). Being and living as a Muslim requires one to acknowledge the spirit contained within the body and soul. Acceptance of belief in the power of the Creator and how life can be led with the mind illuminated with spiritual understanding is a component of being a Muslim.

In Islam, the Creator's benevolence and mercy is offered through reward in the hereafter if one commits one's self to performing good deeds and living righteously. Those who disbelieve, perform evil deeds and do not seek forgiveness are granted hell-fire in the hereafter. These two opposites of eternal existence require Muslims to consciously contemplate their lifestyle choices. Because it is understood that sins may be forgiven but disbelief in the Almighty will not, developing one's spirituality is necessary in order to live in this life and to prepare for the next life.

Perhaps the greatest display of Muslims' understanding of spirituality has been exhibited by the Sufia of Islam. Their love for the Creator and their understanding of the spirit is oft-times expressed in the form of spiritual poetics. Sultan Bahu is a renowned and famous Sufi who ascribed to the belief that if one truly worked in quest of the Lord, prayer and meditation would help guide the soul in its journey to meet Him. He writes:

> Having learned wisdom from a thousand books, they become great scholars. They cannot learn one letter of love—the wretches wander in ignorance. If a lover glances just once, he can swim a hundred million rivers. If the scholar looks a hundred million times, he cannot reach the other bank. Between learning and love is an arduous journey, with many miles of distance. Whoever does not gain love, is a loser in both worlds. (Elias, 1998, p. 48)

Love for the Creator in the form of poetic verse is a remarkable concept perfected by the Sufi. Muslims and non-Muslims alike can learn extensively from what the Sufi teach. According to Sheikh el-Islam Zakaria Ansari, "Sufism teaches how to purify one's self, improve one's morals and build up one's inner and outer life in order to attain perpetual bliss. Its subject-matter is the purification of the soul and its end or aim is the attainment of eternal felicity and blessedness" (Shah, 1970, p. 240). This is the essence of the Sufi way of life. In addition, the unique teachings of the Sufia allow both men and women the possibility of spiritual enlightenment. Treading the Sufi path is not exclusively for men but rather offers spiritual development for human beings in general.

An understanding of what Holy Qur'an, Hadith and the Shariah stipulate about hijab, combined with a spiritual understanding from the Sufi perspective has been explained for the purpose of providing a comprehensive understanding of Islam's beliefs and etiquette directly related to muhajabat. This research seeks to provide an understanding about the experiences of adolescent muhajabat attending public schools. In the quest for deeper understanding of these females, I hypothesized that if there was a concrete understanding of muhajabat based upon Islam's principles of why hijab is worn then these students would receive an educationally and socially improved school environment. As a result, I developed *Hijab Theory*. The purpose of Hijab Theory's formulation is to provide general principles that explain the reasons why muhajabat attending public school veil. This research is also inclusive of a review of literature pertaining to the muhajabat experience, why qualitative research was decided upon, participant interviews and how hijab connects with the administration, teachers and curriculum in public schools. Implications of my findings and the limitations of this study will conclude the research.

CHAPTER II

LITERATURE REVIEW

In this study of muhajabat attending public schools, I explore social and psychological theories and research pertaining to muhajabat. The use of social and psychological theories lends itself to an exploration of psychological and social adaptations of muhajaba while the muhajabat literature provides an example or model of relevant experiences.

I refer to Goffman (1961, 1963, 1967) along with Atkinson, Morten & Sue's (1998) sociological and psychological theories as the grounding theories. The significant relationship between human interaction and social experiences such as stigma, alienation and social identity problems made Goffman's theories vital to this research.

This chapter begins with a review of the literature pertaining to muhajabat and the social and psychological theories used. This is followed by ethnographic research studies applicable to this study. I then systematically investigate the discourses within the multiple research writings and how they relate to this research. I conclude with how my work contributes to the existing muhajabat literature.

Literature Regarding Muhajabat

Rethinking Muslim Women and the Veil (Bullock, 2002), critiques the idea that the veil symbolizes Muslim women's oppression. Bullock (2002) challenges these views of female subjugation by analyzing feminist theory and explaining that their definitions of liberating women are in fact oppressive to some Muslim females. Western feminist views are not universally applicable, and Bullock addresses this issue by looking at the various methodologies of how veiled females are looked upon in the West.

What makes Bullock's work germane to the field is that she is the first Muslim muhajaba to write about the muhajabat experience with a in-depth look at poignant muhajabat issues like feminism and the views that are sometimes promoted such as that women cannot be liberated in Islam and that veiling is equivalent to oppression (pgs. xv-xvi). She also describes experiences Muslims in the West suffer such as indignities like being yelled and sworn at by strangers (pp. 74-75).

Bullock examines the various reasons for wearing hijab, which may include personal preference, custom or even state laws (p. 86) and oppositional views of its necessity for Muslim women. Bullock provides a comprehensive understanding of many of the diverse issues that veiling conjures up while questioning the validity of non-Muslim and, sometimes, Muslim assumptions.

Sarroub (2005) wrote an enthralling account of Muslim Yemeni American girls' experiences. Her book *All American Yemeni Girls, Being Muslim in a Public School* is based in a large Yemeni community in Dearborn, Michigan. She interviewed six muhajabat, grades nine through twelve. The females being interviewed verbally stated that because Sarroub was not Muslim she really did not understand their experiences. As an ethnographer, she was able to examine the strong relationship between these females land of origin and the current place they call home here in the United Stated in relation to what their expectations are and what their families' expectations are for them. It became quite clear that these Yemeni American Muslim girls who wear hijab had numerous identities inclusive of upholding family honor, being a student, becoming wives and, eventually, mothers. This research also brings to light the poignant difference between religion and culture. One example in this book is females being forced to marry someone even if they do not want to, which is expressly forbidden in Islam.

Although Sarroub focused on muhajabat school and home lives, she makes several assumptions. For example, "The fact that the hijabat did not work outside the home and did not participate in after-school activities and sports ensured that they had more than enough time to complete their schoolwork". (p. 112) Many of these females have a lot of home responsibilities such as cooking, cleaning, tutoring siblings, etc. Therefore, whether they are working inside or outside of the homemade little difference in regard to having time for themselves. Crafting a correct opinion of these six Yemeni American Muslim muhajabat is no easy task due to the multi-faceted nature of their realities. Even with the many challenges she faced, Sarroub provided a needed glimpse into the world of the ever-growing group of young muhajabat in the United States.

In *Educating Muslim Girls*, Haw (1998) looked at Muslim female students in both public and private schools and their relationships with teachers. Although the schools that participated in this research were located in the United Kingdom, I believe that most of the research can be generalized to Muslim female students in the United States. She uses both feminist thinking, examining how gender plays a role in shaping the girls' education, as well as post-structuralist theory to shape her analysis, and directly addresses issues of equality and difference within the cultural context of the females she has written about. A key concern that Haw struggled with throughout the text was what causes the subordination of females and how it emerges with the Muslim females in her study. Most informative for my research was the chapter entitled *The Nazrah Story*. Muslim students were given a fictitious character (Nazrah) to write about. The focus was her achievement and experiences in school. After reading the student responses, it was clear that they all individually became Nazrah. They shared feelings and emotions expressing desire for school success and spoke about the racism, isolation, and bullying by peers they encountered. These experiences were not openly discussed in the school community.

Haw concluded that, "What is needed is well theorized practices and practical theories which have the sophistication to deal with 'difference', hybridity and pluralism. This means theories which challenge practice, and practices which challenge theory" (Haw, 1998, p. 182). She demonstrated how we, as educators, should extend our knowledge of theories and their application to school experiences. Then, perhaps, we can make a difference in the lives of students in general, not just the ones we teach. A campus community goal should be tolerance of difference and all members of our community should participate in its development. Muhajabat can be included in achieving the goal of membership in a tolerant community by advocating for their own inclusion, sharing their beliefs and making known their presence. Too often many muhajaba remain separate from the general population for various reasons including feeling stigmatized or like an outcast. Haw believes it is therefore necessary to assist with developing a diverse and respectful school and social environment.

Khanum (1995) authored a chapter in the book *Identity and Diversity* entitled Education and the Muslim Girl. Khanum interviewed Mrs. Mirza, the headmistress of the Bradford Muslim Girls' School in England. She wrote that, "While feminists eschew the hijab and see it as a symbol of oppression, Mrs. Mirza says she feels liberated by it. She claims it makes her feel confident and gives her freedom to move around in the community". (p. 279) Khanum found that many Muslim adolescents and women believe that dressing according to Muslim traditions allows them to be viewed as people and not objects, while others just identify with what they know or understand. She believes it is important that people are comfortable with their beliefs and the choices they make.

Kahf (2006) authored the novel *The Girl in the Tangerine Scarf*. It is based on her experiences of growing up in Indiana as a Syrian, Muslim immigrant. Included in her story are her experiences of being a muhajaba attending a public school. The exuberance in her youth of being a Muslim muhajaba is shared along with the telltale reality of her differences. Kahf recounts an emotional event that occurred in a school hallway where a male student snatched a book from her and yanked her hijab off. "I hate you! She screamed. I hate you! Brent mimicked in falsetto. It's just hair you psycho!" (p. 124). This is an example of the lack of understanding regarding hijab and what it may symbolize to some muhajabat. It is not superficially about 'just covering hair'. Gaining this understanding is possible once the historical and religious teachings regarding hijab are explained.

Negative incidents regarding hijab can affect muhajabat identity. Everyone acts and reacts differently. The experience Kahf encountered left her feeling distraught, but it also seemed to reaffirm and strengthen her desire to continue to wear hijab. "The scarf. It was a mess. She didn't want to give anyone in this building the satisfaction of seeing her bareheaded". (Kahf, 2006, p. 125) She was determined to make it through her day as if it were a normal one. Although Kahf was able to pick up the remnants of her emotions and her hijab, not every muhajaba will be able to do the same thing.

The Girl in the Tangerine Scarf, regardless of the fact that it is based upon an individual's life, provides a glimpse into the experiences that some muhajabat may have while in attendance at a public school. Because the written accounts are shared in the voice of the muhajaba herself, they provide credibility to the belief that researching, discussing and establishing a voice for muhajabat is necessary in academic fields.

Haddad, Smith and Moore wrote about the complexity of the issues Muslim American women face in the West. Their book *Muslim Women in America: The Challenge of Muslim Identity Today* (2006) focuses on aspects of the Muslim faith including stereotypes, conversion to Islam, gender and family issues within the context of the Muslim faith and hijab.

Whenever discussing Islam in America, it is impossible to avoid the topic of hijab because controversy regarding hijab in public schools has been addressed legally in many states in our country. Haddad, Smith & Moore (2006) cite one such incident as an example of school dress code issues involving students in a publicized atmosphere.

> Nashala Hearn, a sixth-grade student at Ben Franklin Science Academy in Muskogee, Oklahoma was suspended twice from school for wearing a religious headscarf, in violation of the school's dress code banning bandanas, hats, and other head coverings. Her parents filed suit against the Muskogee School District in October 2003, and in March 2004 the Justice Department filed a motion in federal court in support of Hearn's position (p. 111).

Muhajabat students being expelled and suspended from public schools is not a new occurrence. Fortunately, these student's experiences are now coming to light because researchers and professors in the academic and social justice arenas are assisting with publicizing their plights.

Muslim Women in America provides insight into the world of Muslim women in the United States and their struggle for educational, political and religious autonomy. It also dispels the notion that Muslim women are not active participants within the societies where they reside.

Overall, I believe this text can assist people attempting to further their knowledge about American Muslim females and their daily experiences, concerns and desires. Nonetheless, there are some assumptions made that as a Muslim and muhajaba I disagree with. For example, the author's state:

> Some women express their allegiance to Islam in very public ways. Rejecting the social norms of Western culture, they try to dress, speak, and live in as close adherence as possible to what they understand to be the dictates of the Qur'an and the traditions of the Prophet. (Haddad, Smith & Moore, 2006, p. 8)

Why would a Muslim female dressing according to her faith be categorized as rejecting the dominant culture where she resides when the United States is continuously referring to itself as a melting pot of cultures? This connotes to me a rather contemplative decision to be different in a society where everyone should 'be the same'. Generally, Muslim females that wear hijab do not look at themselves as different in their country, but rather minorities in their immediate environment. A muhajaba who attends a public school with only one or two other muhajabat are usually with several muhajabat outside of school. There are numerous ideas that have to be considered and taken into perspective when studying the Muslim dress of some Muslim females. Looking through a lens of diversity and multiculturalism where there is an understanding of approval that acknowledges and accepts differences is a beginning. These are the principles that freedom in the United States is supposed to stand for.

In addition, this statement may suggest to some readers that there is a public versus private aspect to Islam. As explained in the introduction, Islam does not separate church and state. "Islam recognizes no division between the religious and the public world". (Weiss, 2000, p. 41) If people, even Muslims, choose to group Islam into various categories, it is simply their choice. It has absolutely nothing to do with Islam's way of life or Islam's teachings.

The authors of *Muslim Women in America* have provided a needed scholarly contribution to the study of Muslim women in the United States. It is both challenging and necessary for Muslim females to have a voice that will oppose their marginalized descriptions and share their social accounts. Other educators and social activists are also participating in this struggle. *Shattering the Stereotypes Muslim Women Speak Out* by Afzal-Khan illuminates the continuous complexities of the Muslim female experience.

Eisa Nefertari Ulen, one of the contributors to this book, authored the chapter *"Tapping Our Strength"* (2005). Ulen's writing is unique and riveting. She writes with introspection and begins by describing her experiences in a Manhattan mosque and the feelings conjured while being there. She speaks candidly about Islam's growth and how she is perceived as a proclaimed Muslim womanist (A woman of African decent whose ideology is grounded in the struggles and experiences of those who share her cultural capital). It is rare to discover females who identify as Muslims write with such surprising strength and vision. As a reader, if there is disagreement with her opinions and beliefs, the uncompromising manner in which she stands by them is admirable. Muhajabat, and growing females in general, need exposure to Muslim women who clarify, stand by and reaffirm their beliefs. Perhaps it will be an incentive to these females to exist and live proudly as they are.

In *Unveiled Sentiments,* Jasmin Zine (2006) examines racism and Islamophobias effects on muhajabat in attendance at a Canadian Muslim school in Toronto where the classes are divided by gender. She explores how these females exist with racial and religious oppression while striving to deal with the sexist and patriarchal forms of oppression stemming from their homes and communities.

Zine discusses the banning of hijab in public schools and particularly focuses on case studies from France and Quebec. The social and political ramifications of hijab banning led to the vilification of Muslim females who practiced veiling as a part of their faith. The debate between public and religious freedom rages until today.

A compelling point made by Zine that I also find true in my own research is that "Stereotypes deny the agency of Muslims who wear the veil, and reduce the multiple meanings associated with the veil to a single negative referant". (Zine, 2006, p. 241) When this occurs in democratic societies, the belief that freedom of religion exists becomes nullified. This reference supports other research about muhajabat in the United States.

Lubna Chaudhry (2005) completed and wrote an ethnographic study of a Pakistani American university student entitled *Aisha and Her Multiple Identities*. When Aisha experienced interactions with a professor that were borderline disrespectful, she spoke with him about how he treated her. He informed her that her hijab made him uncomfortable and no doubt she became increasingly uncomfortable with the reality of her professor's feelings now being made apparent. It is difficult to articulate how a person feels when her presence is reduced to the fact that her hair is not exposed for all to see. It is an overwhelmingly emotional experience that I find difficult to communicate. However, it is probably best explained as a part of ones being or body being perceived as unacceptable.

The stereotypes, discrimination and Islamophobic experiences that muhajabat have to contend with have raised the question of 'Why are so many Muslim females veiling in Western societies'? Ali (2005), author of *Why Here, Why Now? Young Muslim Women Wearing Hijab*, wrote about the increasing number of Muslim females in schools and colleges dressing in Muslim fashions. Ali believes that religion is a form of ethnic identity and that Islam has become more salient in the United States. As a result, he perceives Islam as superseding national and cultural origins that then allows for young women to display their "Muslimness" by wearing hijab. What makes Ali's writing not only interesting but different from other research about the muhajabat experience is his conclusion. Ali declares:

> I argue that the trend toward multiculturalism in this country, with ethnicity becoming a valued and acceptable public form of expression, has created a space where hijab and jilbab, as expressions of a Muslim identity, can flourish (p. 526).

I disagree with this assessment based upon current research, media coverage, national politics and lived experiences. Muhajabat of various ages are experiencing increased racism, discrimination, etc. Social experiences for muhajabat appear to have become more complex and increasingly difficult.

The ethnographic study, *Reconstructing Drop-outs* (Dei, Mazzuca & Zine, 1998), identifies issues that racial or religious minorities experience. These issues may arise when there are problems identifying with the culture and environment. Dei, Mazzuca & Zine state that, "For students who are immigrants from Africa, particularly those from Somalia and Ethiopia, the issues of language, culture, and religion are of utmost concern. Muslim students, in particular, found it easier to formulate an identity through their religion". (p. 158) When asked if expressing his religion as a Muslim had something to do with expressing his individual and cultural identity, Thomas, a Canadian-born twelfth grade student who had converted to Islam two years previously, replied:

> Yes it does because I think . . . I'd like to say it's Islam but perhaps if anyone accepts a new religion and they're into it, then it's going to govern their life . . . at least at the beginning. And Muslims, we're supposed to keep our culture and our identity except if some of that culture clashes with Muslim ideals, right, which isn't a problem with the Black issue. You're a Muslim before you're Black (p. 159).

Dei, Mazzuca & Zine (1997) also directly cited some of the experiences and difficulties faced by Muslim female students that wear hijab. They stated that Muslim students found that: Their religion is not always recognized and validated in schools, both on an ideological level or on a structural level. Some students recalled being outwardly discriminated against by other students, Black and non-Black, on the basis of religious expression. Others, like Thomas, found that while treatment by his friends hadn't changed, he had a sense that stereotypes were being applied to him because of his religious beliefs (pp. 159-160). This study demonstrates that wearing hijab can be a form of religious identity for some and personal expression for others. In today's society this should not be problematic, but as Dei and Zine demonstrate, often it is.

Sociological and Psychological Literature

Goffman's theories regarding identity and human interaction provide an alternate opportunity to examine the experiences of muhajabat attending public schools in New York State. Goffman's research on face-to-face human interaction and identity has provided a major contribution to the field of sociology and contributes to the theoretical framework of this research. Goffman (1963, 1967, 1969) views social interaction as behavior in regular circumstances. He offers an understanding of information gathered through these interactions by examining how individuals perceive themselves and classify others. Goffman also theorizes that when individuals have direct personal contact, symbols and/or signs are used in communication to convey the meaning of these interactions. While socializing, conventional rules are understood so that each individual knows when to respond, speak, or gesture accordingly.

There are different forms of interactions between people, which Goffman terms *gatherings* (1961, p. 18. & 1963, p. 91). These gatherings are of two types: focused and unfocused: "In a focused gathering the participants are organized so that they are maintaining among themselves a jointly sustained focus of attention. In an unfocused gathering no such focus can be discerned and the various participants are pursuing separate lines of concern". (Kendon, 1988, p. 24). Examples of focused gatherings would consist of co-workers conversing while completing a project, an interview or counseling session; and students in classrooms working on lessons and projects. Examples of unfocused gatherings are people in a waiting room or on a grocery store line. At first thought, this may seem to be irrelevant information, but in actuality Goffman was able to identify "A minimal interactive ritual which he termed 'civil inattention' in which passers-by each behaved to the other in such a way that they conveyed, at once, recognition of the passing of another human being and, at the same time, recognition of the other's right to his own, separate, line of action". (Kendon, 1988, p. 25).

Goffman (1967) believes that all human beings participate in interaction rituals, meaning a system of social etiquette between or among people. These rituals could occur between only two people or within an entire group. Individuals focus on a particular occurrence or action and are aware of others having the same focus. A common mood is shared which increases in intensity. He believes that the consequences of these interactions result in the shaping of behavior of those who participate. The intensity of the experience results in the person's emotions and feelings being consciously affected. A person's thoughts or attitudes are produced through their experiences and interactions. These interaction rituals become symbolic of the original experience.

As Collins (1988) describes, people are able to identify who they can turn to for support when an interaction ritual occurs that warrants them needing to be emotionally maintained. He states,

> By means of these symbols people feel where to gravitate for support, where are the centers of power they must respect. On the negative side, they recognize the boundaries of their groups by the lack of respect for their own sacred symbols; and they feel the impulse to punish deviants within their group who demean them symbolically. (p. 45)

There are frames or structures within these interactions whose levels of importance vary and are built upon one another. Their purposes are to show the truth about the structures of a person's experiences. Each level or position begins with primary frameworks, which includes physical objects that people inhabit, their relationships with other people, as well as a person's physical body. At a higher level of these frameworks, an activity can occur which can lead to trying out or practicing an act without committing to it. For example, a Muslim or non-Muslim female may wear hijab in a play, but the Muslim may decide not to wear it every day. Some Muslim females may not have been introduced to or raised with hijab. There are many females who will verbally identify with being Muslim but who cannot cite any reference to hijab in Qur'an or Hadith or even understand any of its origins or Muslim background. Therefore, an activity such as the play mentioned can lead to transformations or changes in a person's nature or character and are symbolic to the person having the experience. Once such an experience is had, interest regarding hijab may be piqued for both Muslims and non-Muslims, which can open the door to research and discovery.

Goffman's theories of social interaction can be applied to an analysis and critique of muhajabat experiences in schools because behaviors and perceptions of muhajabat are constantly developing and changing while they are interacting in their school's environment. Throughout the world, muhajabat are everyday members of society. Within the society or social order, their interactions vary in a multitude of ways and have multiple meanings. I would like to place the experiences of the muhajabat interviewed in this study into the perspective lens of these ritual interactions and within the current climate of educational debate.

In some places this has meant preventing some Muslim females from being allowed to wear hijab in public schools, government buildings, license photographs, etc. As a group without dominant numbers in the larger society, many muhajabat must ask themselves who and where they can locate sources of support that recognize their right to dress according to their personal/religious beliefs. One of the many advantages of living in a 'free' society is the ability to choose when, where, why and how you will interact with anyone. The reality of everyday life in the United States and throughout the world, however, requires individuals to adapt to their circumstances and life's complexities in their everyday interactions.

Symbolic Interaction

Symbolic interactionism is the overall theory developed by Goffman (1969) to explain how people relate to one another and what symbols and actions come into play consciously and unconsciously in their interactions. This theory focuses on the procedures of social interaction, how people feel, observe, describe and analyze one another. Goffman did not develop an approach that explained the theories of interaction but rather focused on analysis of social interaction. As a result of his work, other sociological perspectives related to symbolic interactionism flourished. Hewitt (1997) states that:

> Symbolic interactionism is a distinctively American sociological perspective whose roots lie in the philosophy of pragmatism. Proponents of this approach to philosophy view living things as attempting to make practical adjustments to their surroundings. (p. 7)

This means that symbolic interactionism is specifically oriented to how useful people are when having to conform to a new condition. The regularities of human social life are what interactionists are interested in learning about.

Mead (1982) contributed to the development of symbolic interactionist theory. Goffman's work represents an application of the theory of *symbolic interaction* formulated by Mead. The theory focuses on human action and interaction. Mead refers to human action as society, meaning the actions performed by human beings. Human interaction comprises of society members who engage one another. Symbolic interaction is carried out through gestures and symbols shared between human beings. Symbolic interaction and its components are a part of muhajabat life, just as they are part of anyone else. As muhajabat encounter or experience situations in regard to their dress code, symbolic interaction plays a key role in how other human beings generate meaning, understanding, and act towards these individuals.

Interaction Ritual (Goffman, 1967) was written in a format that breaks social interaction into specific categories to explain human behavior in natural settings. Goffman specifically discussed elements of socialization, embarrassment, alienation, and psychological problems and how they entwine within human interactions. Most applicable to the muhajabat research was Goffman's forms of alienation. Goffman specified four types of alienation that are relevant to the hijab experience:

1. External preoccupation—the outward occupying of one's mind or attention;
2. Self-consciousness—being aware of your own needs so that your own potential can be reached;
3. Interaction-consciousness—to act on one's own existence and environment;
4. Other-consciousness—which is different or distinct from others.

Goffman was able to analyze and interpret social situations. He focused on social construction and the development of the self and has provided a strong sociological orientation for understanding face-to-face interactions that occur between muhajabat and non-muhajabat in public schools.

Schools are places where human interaction occurs throughout the day. Focusing on schools within the framework of symbolic interactionism can expand our understanding of the muhajabat experience as related to public education. Muhajabat identities and behaviors are shaped by their social membership within their educational environments.

Research studies about adolescents in schools and their socialization have also been an important aspect of understanding their identities. Kinney, Rosier & Harger (2003) found that adolescents' social identities are affected by their social interactions in some of the same ways previously explained by symbolic interactionism. They state:

> In general, these studies indicate that distinct peer groups in secondary schools serve as arenas for peer socialization. Membership in specific crowds or categories structures adolescents' every day social interaction and friendship selection. The diverse groups are usually ranked in prestige hierarchy, and their position denotes their relative social status. Moreover, researchers of adolescent socialization processes have found that membership in teenage crowds significantly affects youths' social identities and self-evaluations through processes consistent with symbolic interactionism. (p. 578)

Peer group rankings affect the self-esteem of students, particularly those in the lowest ranking peer groups in contrast to the elite groups. There is an evident hierarchy of adolescent group affiliations.

The muhajabat are a group composed of females of varied ethnic backgrounds with a dress code considered 'different' than that of the mainstream high school students. Symbolic interaction regarding establishing a school social environment in which persons with multiple identities (female, Asian American, Muslim) can converse and interact in a supportive and accepting social environment is important because of these females in public schools and because of the fact that their numbers are increasing. Their presence is an integral and permanent part of the public school environment. It is at this time that Goffman's forms of alienation, (external preoccupation, self-consciousness, interaction-consciousness and other—consciousness) become quite relevant. The education and social environment of the muhajabat is where these four forms of alienation occur.

Symbolic Interaction and Females

There is still a need for conversation to assist in improving the female experience. There are complexities to the female experience that can be analyzed through the symbolic interactionist lens. The worldview of symbolic interaction demonstrates how human potential and interaction blend within our everyday experiences. Focusing on the muhajabat experience, symbolic interaction allows us to narrow our scope to what is specific and relevant to them and pinpoint the social needs of these females.

It is clear that gender and identity shape one another:

> To symbolic interactionists, gender is learned social behavior associated with each anatomical sex. It is a social classification. Every person (or actor) is taught the meanings for gendered behavior. Each person, in turn, teaches it to others. Gender involves more than simply learning masculine or feminine behavior. It also involves the entire person in the process of becoming human. (Deegan 1987, p. 4)

This means that males and females learn behavior that they in turn teach others and that these behaviors result in being categorized and accepted as masculine or feminine. The relationship between symbolic interaction and females can help explain the muhajabat experience, which can be further understood and analyzed through a framework of interpretation: "The symbolic interactionist framework states that learning to take the standpoint of others toward oneself begins in interpersonal relations within primary groups (e.g., the family, neighborhood play group, school peer groups)". (Kinney, Rosier & Harger 2003, p. 577) Realizing their differences in the context of the public school environment, some muhajabat use a degree of thought about how they are perceived by teachers and fellow students. They then attempt to place the teacher or students at ease by connecting with them in some way. For example, a muhajaba wearing a red blouse would say to another student wearing the same color, "nice shirt". The comment is meant to signify that they have something in common and hopefully work to place the student at ease with the muhajaba's obvious difference, i.e. wearing a form of Muslim attire (hijab). Some muhajabat are aware that their appearance creates discomfort in others regardless of whether or not they understand the reasons.

Social Identity

Goffman believes that when we come in contact with strangers, their first appearance causes us to anticipate what they are like. "We lean on these anticipations that we have, transforming them into normative expectations, into righteously presented demands". (Goffman, 1963, p. 2) According to Goffman, we do not realize that we have made assumptions until after the demands we place upon people are fulfilled or unfulfilled. A person's real or actual social identity is the attributes he or she possesses irrespective of whether or not other people know they possess them. The actual social identity of Muslim females that wear hijab may, therefore, be difficult for others to discover. When people unfamiliar with Muslims come into contact with a muhajabat, they may be uncomfortable initiating contact or conversation. As a result, those individuals may cling to the preconceived notions or ideas that they already possess regarding muhajabat.

Vryan, Adler and Adler (2003) concede that "Our social identities result from identification of us (by self and others) with socially constructed groups or categories of people, or our positions within social structures". (p. 369) A muhajaba's social identity may be defined by Muslims as similar to other muhajaba and may be easily differentiated from those who do not share the same religious and social identity. It is easier for one muhajaba to talk and share with another muhajaba about the constraints related to their socialization and feelings about their social experiences than it may be to talk to a non-muhajaba.

A stigma is an assigned negative attribute or failing that constitutes a part of identity. Muhajabat are sometimes marred by stigma in Western societies and considered abnormal. Goffman (1963) identifies three types of stigma; abominations of the body, blemishes of individual character, and tribal stigma of race, nation and religion. (p. 4) Muhajabat can be placed in the category Goffman terms 'tribal stigma'. Tribal stigmas can occur through lineage via race, religion or nation. In the United States, muhajabat may be stigmatized due to the obvious religious difference between them and those considered 'normal'. Muhajabat do not look upon one another as persons with a stigma. To the contrary, stigma amongst muhajabat may, however, occur within the immediate families if an individual chooses to stop wearing hijab when she is a member of a family where this is expected or if a person begins to wear hijab and they are a member of a Muslim family that does not wear hijab.

Tribal stigma can affect all family members. Persons with a stigma are usually discriminated against by those society deems normal. Discrimination and prejudice are closely linked. When Lynch (1987) defines prejudice and discrimination, he states that:

> Prejudice, or its correlates, racism, sexism, credism, and
> classism, is the subjective belief in the superiority of one's
> own grouping (or gender) over other peoples. Discrimination
> occurs when these passive behaviors are translated into
> the active mode so that individuals are denied legitimate
> opportunity, reward or resource on the basis of another
> person's prejudiced attitudes. (p. 25)

Stigma incorporates prejudice and discrimination by allowing an individual who is different to be prejudged and to feel his or her differences in comparison to a person considered normal. A key feature of the stigmatized person's life is that it is enshrouded with the need for acceptance. When stigmatized persons realize the relationship between their stigma and the status of their social identity, they may attempt to change the attribute that is marring their acceptance.

Goffman's book *Stigma: Notes on the Management of Spoiled Identity* (1963), focuses on people as individuals and the difficulties they face trying to fit into what is considered *normal* (acceptable to the majority) society. He shows how disqualification from normalcy in Western society may come from rare physical abnormalities or differences in race, religion or social class in contrast to the majority population. These differences may result in the individual's self—image being negatively affected. Goffman explores how individuals cope with these experiences and their altering identities. This work is important to my own research because it provides a base to analyze the experiences of muhajaba in their educational social settings from a sociological perspective. Muhajabat bear the stigma or unwanted mark of being individuals wearing veils in an environment where the majority of people are unveiled. Their relationship with those deemed *normal* or conforming to a typical standard requires close scrutiny in order to gather a comprehensive understanding of their reality.

Although Goffman provides a thorough understanding of social acceptance, there is an assumption that a stigma remains a stigma when this is not necessarily the case. A muhajaba may suffer discrimination due to being stigmatized based on her appearance. This may occur in a school, the mall, or any other social setting. The question becomes, does the stigma remain the same if the muhajaba is in the mall alone in contrast to being in the mall with six other muhajabat? How 'normals' perceive the muhajaba may remain the same in either circumstance, but if it is different for the muhajaba depending on these factors, then being stigmatized or feeling stigmatized may differ. In this case, theories of interaction ritual are beneficial to gain a further understanding of how stigmatized persons may act or react depending on their environment.

Stigma and Group Representation

As a muhajaba, people who continuously come into contact with me usually ask questions or make statements such as: 'I didn't know you could wear a colored scarf. I thought you had to wear black or white. Do not 'they' usually make you wear black or white?' I am expected to give an answer, which usually is quite lengthy. I have to explain that Muslim females are individuals, and that some may choose to wear what they want based on their own likes, dislikes, beliefs, family structure, etc. Most importantly, there is no possible way that I can speak for all muhajabat and their hijab style and color. It becomes difficult feeling that I am required to answer questions about a particular category or group with which I am affiliated. When this occurs, I find solace in discussing it with other muhajabat. Like other individuals with a stigma, I get support from those who share the same experience: "a new career is likely to be thrust upon him, that of representing his category". (Goffman, 1963, p. 26) This is a reality from which stigmatized persons are unable to escape.

Stigma and Alienation

Living with a stigma can be a very damaging and hurtful reality. Stigmatized individuals may withdraw from interacting with others to preserve their self-respect. For example, a muhajaba eating lunch in the school cafeteria who hears students snickering or making jokes about her hijab may withdraw from eating lunch in the cafeteria environment or she may confront those she believes are causing her discomfort. The muhajaba choosing to withdraw from the environment perhaps experiences feelings of alienation and makes a choice not to be placed in an uncomfortable social situation.

Alienation is quite relevant to interaction and socialization. Goffman (1967, pp. 117-121) identifies four forms: external preoccupation, self-consciousness, interaction—consciousness, and other-consciousness. In external preoccupation, the individual is concerned with something that is not being addressed at that specific moment in time. "The object of the individual's preoccupation may be one that he ought to have ceased considering upon entering the interaction, or one that is to be appropriately considered only later in the encounter or after the encounter has terminated". (Goffman, 1967, p. 117) An example of this would be a muhajaba who was ridiculed in gym class by a student. In an English class that takes place after gym, the muhajaba is still focused on the incident that did not take place in English. Any interaction the muhajaba has with other students in the English class is separate from the gym class occurrence yet affected by it. Self-consciousness is when an individual focuses unnecessary attention upon himself instead of engaging in the conversation at hand. During this self-conscious time the individual is seeking some sort of response, whether positive or negative, from others. In contrast to self-consciousness, interaction consciousness is when an individual is concerned with how a conversation is proceeding and as a result the individual does not participate in the interaction. Other-consciousness occurs with interaction when "The individual may become distracted by another participant as an object of attention-exactly as in the case of self-consciousness he can become distracted by concern over himself". (Goffman, 1967, p. 120) The individual may feel that the others involved in the conversation are causing him/her to be overly conscious. When this occurs, the individual may begin to identify people he or she believes are being insincere and attempts to control how those individuals view him or her.

Research Literature

There is research applicable to the experiences of muhajabat. Hallet (2003) references Goffman and uses his interactional theories to formulate a model aiding in understanding how emotions play a role in social interaction. His research about emotional feedback and social interaction and his findings can be contrasted with the muhajabat experience. "In the modern era, Goffman linked emotions to particular types of interactions". (Hallet, 2003, p. 706) If the current issues pertaining to muhajabat are observed, one may find this to be true. Whether it is due to the global political climate, war, or racism and discrimination, the hijab worn by Muslim females evokes reactions expressing the growing intolerance towards Muslims in the United States. Emotions linked to these interactions become obvious and are further explained by Hallet when he states, "Sometimes we bumble into interactions with little purpose, but these interactions still have consequences for our emotions, and feedback and amplification can occur in either spontaneous or managed interactions". (2003, p. 708) When someone closely follows the American-Iraq war and is presented with visual images of muhajabat, feedback and response will occur based on that individual's emotional response and influence his or her interactions.

Reactive and participatory forms of appeasement are the focus of the article *Appeasement in Human Emotion, Social Practice and Personality.* Keltner, Young & Buswell (1997) review the process of human appeasement. Embarrassment and shame are reactive forms of human appeasement, and modesty and shyness are anticipatory. Appeasement which "begins when the conditions of social relations lead one individual to aggression from others, is expressed in submissive, inhibited behavior, which in turn evokes inferences and emotions in others that bring about social reconciliation" (Keltner, Young & Buswell, 1997, p. 359). Examples of this would be embarrassment and shame which are reactive, and modesty and shyness, which are anticipatory.

In their analysis of appeasement, the researchers apply Goffman's theories of social interaction, which includes modesty as a strategy. Modesty is believed to be a category of politeness and proper social etiquette. Goffman believes that polite modesty is a way of bestowing respect and honor upon others. As a result, social harmony is increased which in turn achieves the goal of appeasement. The article concludes by identifying various appeasement functions of shyness, polite modesty, etc, and stating that emotions and social interactions that promote social relationships are performed through appeasement. This is also relevant to muhajabat who deem modesty as a requirement of Muslim social behavior but who will nonetheless alter their hijab or their Muslim clothing in order to participate in a harmonious school atmosphere.

In *Towards an Embodied Understanding of the Structure/Agency Relationship,* Shilling (1999) describes the structure/agency relationships and its limitations. According to Shilling, "The 'interaction order' identifies the embodied dimensions of interaction as consequential for, yet irreducible to, structures and agents, enables us to investigate the 'loose coupling' of interaction to individuals and social systems, but is underdeveloped in important respects". (Shilling, 1999, p. 543) The two significant limitations of this theory are:

1. Emotional dimensions of human interaction and socialization are marginalized;
2. There are inadequacies when people and the social system are being examined due to lack of understanding about the significance of their interplay.

Shilling references Goffman's 'interaction order' to provide an understanding of the importance of social interaction and face-to-face relations. Relevant to this order are the moral demands that are placed upon people: "As Goffman's (1952) writings on deceit illustrate, people may have a need for a social self, but are not forced to act in particular ways. If they betray the trust which maintains this order, however, their social identity becomes 'tainted' ". (Shilling, 1999, p. 546)

Pertaining to muhajabat, an example of tainted social identity may be when one must remove the hijab in order to attend school. Those who buckle under the pressure or choose to remove their veil to achieve their educational needs and goals will possibly promote alienation between themselves and those who refuse to be religiously inconspicuous. Their social identity may be mobilized in the educational environment but damaged in the home, religious, or every day social settings. In this type of situation, human interaction and socialization becomes overwhelmingly significant. The effects of the interaction help us to understand the interplay between individuals and their social systems.

In addition to sociological studies, there is psychological research also applicable to the muhajabat experience. Atkinson, Morten and Sue are psychologists who work in the field of counseling. Their primary focus has been cross-cultural perspectives on counseling American minorities, particularly African-Americans, Native-Americans, Asian-Americans and Latin—Americans. Their goal has been sensitizing counselors to the needs of minority groups and their cultural differences. They examine counseling failure and seek to change the counseling field through ethnic and minority group education and understanding. Although their research and findings are specific to counseling, I believe that much of their work parallels some of the muhajabat experiences pertaining to self-awareness, cultural belief differences and values, and how minorities feel about or deal with issues or concerns that arise in social interactions.

Atkinson, Morten & Sue (1998) use the Minority Identity Development Model (MID Model) to assist counselors in understanding the behaviors and attitudes of the people they service. Through the use of the MID Model, they hope to understand the individual's relationship with his or her own culture and also with the dominant culture that they sometimes struggle to be a part of and understand. The MID Model consists of five stages:

1) Conformity—self-deprecating attitude.
2) Dissonance—conflicting self-attitude between self-deprecating and appreciating.
3) Resistance and immersion—self-appreciating.
4) Introspection—concern with the basis of self-appreciation.
5) Synergetic—self-appreciating, articulation and awareness.

In the conformity stage, "Minorities view themselves as deficient in the desirable characteristics held up by the dominant society. Feelings of racial self-hatred caused by cultural racism may accompany this type of adjustment". (Atkinson, 1998, p. 36) Denial is a component of this stage. Deterioration of their denial system occurs in the dissonance stage, while the resistance and immersion stage consists of an individual rejecting dominant group culture and endorsing the views of their own group. At this stage the individual strives to eliminate oppression and other ills that his or her group faces. In the introspection stage, individuals have become comfortable with their identity. Questions about the positive or negative belief or experiences as regard the dominant culture arise: "In the introspection stage of development, the minority individual experiences feelings of discontent and discomfort with group views rigidly held in the Resistance and Immersion stage and diverts attention to notions of greater individual autonomy". (Atkinson, Morten & Sue 1998, pp. 38-39) The synergistic or final stage is when an individual's cultural identity feels complete, accepted and fulfilled. At this stage, the individual accepts or rejects the cultural values of their own group and/ or the dominant group after careful consideration. The decision is based on experiences in the previous stages of identity development.

The Minority Identity Development Model may easily be applied to muhajabat and their experiences. The inability to live up to the dominant group, resistance to assimilation, and feelings of discontent are all examples of similarities between the MID Model and muhajabat experiences. The problem with the MID Model and how it applies to some muhajabat is the sequence of the theory's stages. Although the stages of the model may apply at one point or another to some muhajabat, there may be no specific order that each muhajaba will go through all five stages in the way proposed by the MID Model. Human experiences are varied and dependent on multiple factors and it is possible for a muhajaba to skip a particular stage or experience them in different orders.

Just as Atkinson, Morten & Sue believe that therapy with African Americans must be consistent with their worldview, respectful and non-racist, so too must socializing and educating muhajabat. There are five issues that Atkinson, Morten and Sue believe a culturally sensitive counselor/teacher needs to consider:

1) Historical perspectives (what values are imparted by family?);
2) Current and historical social support system (how do they deal with oppression and racism?) Support usually comes from family and religious affiliation;
3) Unique characteristics of the value system (spirituality and respect for one's elders is high on the value system list for African Americans and for Muslims as well as African—Americans);
4) Communication barriers (due to cultural differences or variations, miscommunication may occur between the counselors or teachers and the individual);
5) Strategies for effectiveness (for counseling or services to be effective, many things should be taken into consideration. For example, the individual's current experiences and how personal values affect conduct, considering spiritual values and being flexible when dealing with individuals).

Cultural sensitivity is not only important for the white teacher or therapist, but for minorities who also may have preconceived notions and ideas about European Americans. This is something that all of us must recognize: "We construct a stigma-theory, an ideology to explain his inferiority and account for the danger he represents, sometimes rationalizing an animosity based on other differences, such as those of social class". (Goffman, 1963, p. 5)

Atkinson and Morten also discuss children of mixed marriages and their lack of firm self—identities: "As social outcasts they exist between two cultures and are not allowed close to the social center of either group to become 'whole' selves" (Foeman & Nance 1999, p. 547). Contrasting this view with the experiences of muhajabat in the United States may allow us to further explore the importance of multiple identities and connects with Goffman's theories of stigma and spoiled identity.

> By definition, of course, we believe the person with a stigma is not quite human. On this assumption we exercise varieties of discrimination, through which we effectively, if often unthinkingly reduce his life chances. We construct a stigma—theory, and ideology to explain his inferiority and account for the danger he represents, sometimes rationalizing an animosity based on other differences, such as those of social class. We use specific stigma terms such as cripple, bastard, moron, in our daily discourse as a source of metaphor and imagery, typically without giving thought to the original meaning. (Goffman, 1963, p. 5)

If we add muhajaba to the list of stigma terms, it becomes easier to see how undesired attributes are linked to a group or individual without the original meaning being sought out or correctly defined. In turn, people become defensive about being perceived as having some sort of defect. Their self-identity then bares a burdensome stigma.

Shonfeld-Ringel (2001) addresses the relationship between European American therapists and their Asian clients. This work is pertinent to muhajabat because it highlights the importance of categorizing all non-muhajabat as being unsympathetic to their muhajabat experiences. The premise of this particular paper is that the working alliance of muhajabat should be expanded by the inclusion of certain domains. "These domains are empathy, mutuality, the dynamics of power and authority, the use of self, and process of communication". (p. 53)

Empathy is understanding or identifying with another person's feelings. In cross-cultural treatment, there is another component: accepting multiple realities of the client whether personal or cultural.

I believe mutuality is important to both the counselor-client and teacher-student relationship because what each brings to the situation and how they interact is of grave importance. With the dynamics of power and authority, being aware of the power and authority the therapist, counselor, or teacher may have over the client is essential. Shonfeld-Ringel states:

> While the White social worker may believe in equalizing the relationship with the minority client, and in basing their practice on principles of collaboration, traditional Asian cultures are more hierarchical, and the therapist is typically viewed as an authority and as an expert. (Shofeld-Ringel, 2001, p. 55)

Contextualizing this with muhajabat experiences, teachers and school administrators have to be aware that the muhajabat students may not share information vital to their educational experience out of respect for the teacher or school administrators' authority. Complaining or reporting adverse school experiences is considered by some to place a burden on those in authority. A grin-and-bear-it mentality is prevalent amongst some muhajabat, depending on their cultural backgrounds. As a result, mutuality becomes an important constituent of understanding the muhajabat school experience.

The use of self refers to the therapist analyzing and critiquing his or her own experiences and using them as a therapeutic tool. Communication in the counselor-client relationships is both verbal and non-verbal. Because non-verbal communication may have different meanings for Americans and Asians, Shonfeld-Ringel refers to Sue's example, "the client's silence may mean a hesitation to disagree with the therapist out of respect for authority and appreciation for harmony, rather than because of over-compliance" (Shonfeld-Ringel, 2001, p. 56). Whether teaching, counseling or interacting with minorities socially, understanding each domain and their applicability to these individuals may assist in creating a framework that fosters improved understanding.

Muhajabat can be categorized as minorities in the United States even if they do not perceive themselves as such. Experiences of different minorities may differ in some aspects but are similar in other respects. For example, an African American muhajaba may experience anti—Muslim and racist interactions while an African American female who is not a muhajaba may experience racism. *Counseling American Minorities* (1998) describes why it is necessary for counselors to understand the need for cultural sensitivity in the counselor-client relationship and clearly recognize that client diversification is and will continue to grow. Contrasting counseling minorities with educating minorities in public schools elicits similar needs and trends. Minority students need teachers who have been prepared in their teacher education courses to teach diverse student populations. Basically, "Taking into account, in their teaching, the diversity of cultural backgrounds of all learners, teachers need to seek ways which will afford all children equity and equality of educational opportunity". (Lynch, 1987, p. 3) This is a goal that all educators should have and be working towards diligently.

Morality and Education

When discussing human interactions, in this case interaction between muhajabat and the public school population, the focus must be on how muhajabat are perceived and treated while interacting. An environment that signifies to them that they will be respected and cared for is an ingredient necessary for their school success. Noddings, an educator who advocates the importance of caring in academia has written extensively about this subject.

She believes teaching morals and ethical behavior can improve human life and that moral education would improve school curricula by displaying to students how a moral foundation can positively improve their lives. Her goal is for schools to assist in laying a moral foundation for the students to take with them once leaving the educational environment. Noddings' moral education differs from character education: "In contrast to views that emphasize reasoning, problem-solving, and critical thinking, character education concentrates on the development of virtues". (Noddings, 2002, p. 61) Moral education has various components. It focuses on modeling caring, open-ended dialogue, and practice in being a caregiver. This model is based on an ethical principle that all human beings want to be cared for.

I do not believe that the 'care theory' is without defect. The problem I have is its dependence on people being taught to be good. No one person learns anything in the exact same manner. If muhajabat have to wait for students that interact with them to be trained to be good to them, the question arises, what effect does waiting have on these muhajabat? The diversity amongst human beings is as broad as the human experience. The endeavor to promote caring can be appreciated even if not easily achieved. Noddings acknowledges that there are pitfalls with care theory and that there are no guarantees, but she does not seem to be overly concerned about this fact when it comes to realistically critiquing whose 'good' will be the standard in promoting caring and what happens during the space of time when a person does not care about their fellow student being respected or treated well.

Noddings' *Educating Moral People* (2002) is quite different from *Caring* (1984). In *Caring,* she examines the why and how of care and in *Educating Moral People,* Noddings focuses on how the caring model can be incorporated in education. I appreciate Nodding's views in *Caring* because she explains the importance of having regard and affection for others. This concept of caring is essential for muhajabat who in many circumstances are categorized as 'others'. The caring model allows for differences between people while providing them with the ability to be different when it comes to their beliefs, views, interests and experiences. Caring allows one human being to consider other human beings' desires and feelings. It is essential that the caring person helps the cared for to achieve self-actualization and growth.

The concept of caring has many merits but is not without problems. There are situations where a person may not care, and there is also the inability to care for people outside of one's reach or surrounding environment. There is no one answer as to how to resolve these problems. If we are aware of them the challenge is then emphasizing the importance of caring to the extent possible. Much like the muhajabat experience, there is no one answer. Nevertheless, realizing that the muhajabat experience is a relevant issue to education is the first step towards assisting these females in whatever educational and social challenges they are facing. Without acknowledgement, the muhajabat issue as it pertains to public education will not be addressed.

Spirituality and Education

Teaching morality, ethics and caring in schools raises the question of spirituality and its place in education. The methods of morality and caring promoted by Noddings (1984), are not interchangeable with spirituality. There are various meanings of the word *spirituality*. I will use Dr. Samuel Johnson's definition: "Acts independent of the body; pure acts of the soul; mental refinement" (Jones, 1986, p. xxiv). Spirituality refers to a living being's purest feelings within their minds and souls. Spirituality does not define the religious preference of individuals but rather compliments their faith, principles, and entire being.

Spirituality in education involves providing students with an educational environment that supports connections to their inner being. It may have nothing to do with promoting a particular religion, but rather encourages individuals to identify what they believe is sacred and use it to address difficulties, hopefully resulting in positive ideals, values, and a sense of well being. There is no definitive marker indicating when spirituality in education became an issue of concern but currently it is a subject of much thought by educators and sociologists regarding its benefits to students (Garrison, 2002; Lantieri; 2001 & Tisdell 2003).

Conversations about spiritual values and morals have increased in intensity over the past few years. The growing number of violent incidents in public schools have brought the issue of spirituality in education to the forefront. Religion and religious practices are not accepted in public schools. Therefore, spirituality or spiritual values have not been promoted due to the belief by some that religion and spirituality are synonymous. Spiritual values or moral growth and development in public schools are, however, of utmost importance to some parents and students who attend these schools. Whether or not the goal is to achieve decreased violence in schools or acceptance of muhajabat or other minority groups, caring plays an important role. There is no exclusivity in ethical and moral education. A person in school, home, at their religious place of worship, or in their community, can practice moral and ethical caring. It allows for positive nurturing and respect for human life.

In elementary schools across the United States, there are currently character, moral, and/or ethical education curriculum programs being implemented and used. Many of these programs earned federal funding through the United States' Department of education in the 1990's:

> In response to the perceived need for schools to address problems with students' character, the U.S. Department of Education's Office of Educational Research and Improvement (OERI) funded character initiatives in the latter half of the 1990's. (Smagorinsky & Taxel, 2005, p. xv)

Nonetheless, high schools, whether due to time constraints or more focused academic standards, appear to neglect the importance and necessity of moral and ethical education. Noddings (2002) writes that, "All children must learn to care for other human beings, and all must find an ultimate concern in some center of care: care for self, for intimate others, for associates and acquaintances, for distant others, for animals, for plants and the physical environment, for objects and instruments, and for ideas" (p. 94). Making moral and ethical education a priority, we allow for improved student-peer relationships, schools, and communities. We achieve human acceptance irrespective of whether an individual is a muhajaba, Arab, Asian or American.

Current Themes in Muhajabat Literature

Themes inclusive of current muhajabat literature are redundant. However, current themes include:

1) The necessity to develop a tool to assist in understanding muhajabat;
2) Public schools are being challenged with cultural diversity and multicultural issues;
3) Power and privilege explored in relation to the muhajabat experience.

Bullock (2002) provided an introduction in *Rethinking Muslim Women and The Veil* inclusive of how the hijab has been seen as a tool of oppression. Bullock espouses that she herself once believed the veil to be a symbol of Muslim oppression. In the introduction she briefly glossed over the fact that many Muslims believe veiling to be theologically supported by Muslim teachings. Prior to Bullock accepting Islam as her religion and faith, she stated that, "I was shown the verses in the Qur'an that many Muslims believe enjoin covering on men and women, and it seemed quite clear to me then that, indeed, the versus did impose covering". (Bullock, 2002, p. XIII). Bullock continues her writings by analyzing the feminist approaches to critiquing veiling used by Muslims and non-Muslims alike. She sets forth various ways in which the veil is critiqued by feminists and believes it is difficult to categorize the views of liberal feminists.

Bullock (2002) acknowledges discourses that emerged in the 1990's that includes separate but related unusual occurrences. That is, anthropologists studying the characterization of Muslim females and Muslim feminists that demand an indigenous feminism. "By and large, it seems that many feminists have trouble knowing how to deal with the veil, Islam, and the women who embrace it". (Bullock, 2002, p. XXIII) Indigenous feminism would provide a tool to understand muhajabat based upon who they are.

Central to Bullock's writing is the focus on hijab in the colonial era. Bullock discovered that by the eighteenth century, Europeans believed veiling was an oppressive custom practiced by Muslims and it eventually became ammunition utilized by European colonizers of the Middle East. The European fantasy of saving Muslim women and sparing, an elusive and unfulfilled desire, continues to have effects on European and Western societies today.

Bullock's (2002) writing is a comprehensive compilation of manifold issues referencing the muhajabat experience in every day life. These include: feminist approaches to the veil, hijab in the colonial era, multiple meanings of hijab and alternative theories regarding hijab. Although she intimates important elements of the muhajabat experience, she does not specifically focus on muhajabat within the public and public school arena.

In contrast, Sarroub (2005) explicitly looked at the experiences of Yemeni American muhajabat attending public school in Dearborn, Michigan. She frames these females' discourses by taking into account the relationship between their religion, gender, nationality, family and education. The distinctiveness of this study derives from Sarroub's ability to examine closely a group of muhajabat students about who very little has been written.

Sarroub (2005) does not delve into the religious teachings pertaining to hijab, rather she focuses on the experiences of the growing Muslim population at the school where her research is conducted. The number of Muslims residing in Dearborn is increasing, as is the Muslim student populous which was forty percent at the high school when Sarroub was completing her fieldwork.

All American Yemeni Girls (Sarroub, 2005) differs from other writings about muhajabat school students because it is specific to the Yemeni culture and, therefore, may not be transferable to muhajabat as a larger group. The author also looks at the role of the public school administration and teachers who face the difficulties associated with cultural pluralism and its effects on the learning environment. Sarroub (2005) analyzes the way in which the school dealt with tensions between various school groups and in the community. She is one of the very few to give credence to an influential function (the arduous relationship between culture, religion and education) of the public education community of which muhajabat are members.

Haw (1998) examines the relationships between muhajabat and their predominately white and non-Muslim teachers. She focuses on how feminist discourse relates to equality and difference in an all-girls' public school as well as a private Muslim girls' school. Haw is one of the first educational researchers to eagerly focus on muhajabat in both a public and private school setting.

The primary goal of *Educating Muslim Girls* (Haw, 1998) was to study white privilege in relation to teacher and Muslim student relationships. Haw began by questioning her own purpose as a white, non-Muslim woman writing about this topic. She concluded that there was a need for a discourse that would acknowledge issues of power and how it correlates with race and gender. I paralleled Haw's stated intention to, "open up spaces for critical dialogue and for the 'voices' of Muslim women" (Haw, 1998, p. 4) in one of my own research purposes.

Feminist theory has been used to learn about and understand the causation and results of women's subordination. My concerns regarding using feminism as a theoretical foundation for my research resurfaced when reading Haw's words that state:

> I resist being placed in any one feminism because I feel
> unable to locate myself in one perspective which holds true

at all times for all issues. The perspective which I do adopt is one which holds onto commonalities and fragmentations, in the belief that there are times when difference should not be exaggerated because the similarities are more important and vice versa. (1998, p. 16)

I believe that structuring my research around Goffman's (1967) social theory provides a critical foundation that furthers understanding regarding muhajabat and their social and school experiences. Although Haw's research was completed in the United Kingdom, I believe her exploration and findings are applicable to Muslim, female school students and muhajabat all over the world.

This research contributes to the existing body of literature about females who wear hijab and extends the knowledge base pertaining to muhajabat by addressing three distinctive characteristics:

1. Islam's point of view regarding hijab;
2. A theory distinct from what has been used before upon which to ground muhajabat experience;
3. The significance of stigma and social identity as it relates to the muhajabat experience. I seek to minimize the disparity in literature regarding muhajabat by providing research that adopts novel perspectives about their experiences. The following chapter focuses on the system of procedures and principles that were applied in this research.

CHAPTER III

METHODOLOGY

Introduction

This chapter focuses on the methodology used to investigate the experiences of muhajabat in their school environment. My desire to closely examine these experiences and emphasize the descriptions of what these muhajabat encounter, combined with investigating what meanings they derive from these social occurrences were the primary reasons I chose to use qualitative research techniques for this research (Bryman, 1999). Redefining and regenerating ideas to further understandings about the research topic is challenging, but once findings are concluded, factual information beneficial to understanding the muhajabat issue can be achieved.

Purpose

This research examines the experiences of muhajabat students in attendance at public high schools and colleges using qualitative research methods. Qualitative research is advantageous when the goal is to discover deep and meaningful information (Seidman, 1998). It allows me to ask the questions: 'What can we learn from this person and their experiences?' and 'How can this information be shared to educate others?' Studying the experiences of muhajabat will therefore allow us to understand the practices and meanings of their customs, culture, and religion from their own perspective. As Eder and

Fingerson (2002) wrote, "One clear reason for interviewing youthful respondents is to allow them to give voice to their own interpretations and thoughts rather than rely solely on our adult interpretations of their lives". (p. 181) This will help us understand how their educational experiences effect their identity and personal development, as well as what the complexities of their identity formations are. My research endeavors include discovering how muhajabat exist in a public school environment as students, how they view themselves, how they would like to be viewed by peers and teachers, and how and why they identify with other muhajabat.

The Research Question

The purpose of this study is to investigate the experiences of muhajabat by answering the question, "How can females adhering to the Muslim head dress (hijab) succeed in public schools and what can be learned from their educational and social experience?" Qualitative research facilitated the answering of this question.

Qualitative research can be defined as descriptions in words (verbal and written) that explore social meanings. According to Bryman & Burgess (1999), qualitative research is a strategy of social research whose characteristics include: "The interpretation of social phenomena from the point of view of the meanings employed by the people being studied; the deployment of natural rather than artificial settings for the collection of data; and generating rather than testing theory". (p. x) This chapter includes the objectives of qualitative research and methods utilized in this study, along with data collection and analysis with subsections including: interviews, direct observation, and photographs and surveys.

Objective of Qualitative Research

Muhajabat in the United States may experience challenges comparative to one another, however, their views are not necessarily one and the same. The experiences of these females vary due to age, race, socio-economic status, ethnicity, family life, religious practices and a spectrum of other factors. Being female may begin to have a more complex definition for some once Muslim and muhajaba are added.

Understanding this requires knowledge about what these females experience.

Interviewing as Qualitative Research (Seidman, 1998) is an excellent tool for the purpose of furthering analysis of the muhajabat experience. Reading this text prior to conducting this research awakened me to my express purpose for interviewing which was also highlighted in the beginning of Seidman's book. He declared that,

> The purpose of in-depth interviewing is not to get answers to questions, nor to test hypotheses, and not to 'evaluate' as the term is normally used. At the root of in—depth interviewing is an interest in understanding the experience of other people and the meaning they make of that experience. (p. 3)

I wanted the students I interviewed to understand that I felt their stories are of worth. I knew from the beginning that their stories and experiences would not be synonymous with my own, but I wanted to come to some conclusion about what I could do to make people aware of their plight.

Maxwell authored *Qualitative Research Design* (1996). I used his interactive model of research design to guide my work. It is beneficial because he lists what questions researchers should address and think about for each of the five components. These components interconnect with one another and are not linear. They help to identify the implications of my research while acknowledging the connections the components have with one another. He utilized this method in his text and demonstrated its effective use. My own model included:

1. Purpose—To bring forth and recognize the issues that Muslim females wearing hijab and attending public schools face;
2. Conceptual Context—I developed a theory that I term 'Hijab Theory' which draws on Muslim females who wear hijab and on their educational experiences and social interactionism. The existing research of Zine (2006), Bullock (2002) and Haw (1998) will be drawn upon to further understand the experiences of muhajabat attending public schools.

3. Interview Questions—How do you feel about being a muhajaba in public school? What are some of the experiences you have had, which you would deem positive or negative? How can teachers and principals assist muhajabat in having an improved educational experience?;
4. Methods—To better understand what the people interviewed are feeling. Information resulting from the interviews is discussed in subsequent chapters;
5. Surveys—To share a wider sampling of opinions with regard to the muhajabat experience;
6. Observations—To compare what they share during the interviews and to form a more comprehensive understanding of their experiences.
7. Photographs—Provide visual representations. They make the research 'real' for some people;
8. Implications & Findings—These I based on explanations, feelings, opinions, etc. of the people who participated in interviews. They are potentially challenging due to the diversity of what muhajabat experienced individually. In these types of situations, there are no right answers but rather various answers that may lend themselves to improving the educational and social experiences of muhajabat.

LeCompte and Schensul demonstrated, in *Analyzing & Interpreting Ethnographic Data* (1999), how charts, diagrams, and numbers can enable us to appropriately interpret research data. Although qualitative research is my preference, I appreciated the comparison chart of inductive analytic strategies. This research was inductive in that I had to discover what would emerge after I had begun. I knew that I would not be able to start out with a particular theme. Using this text allowed me to focus on what strategy would be most useful to this effort. I identified Lofland's (LeCompte & Schensul, 1999) analysis from the suggested strategies as the one best aligned with what I was doing. The inductive analytic strategies include identifying: participants, their activities, their social settings, and their patterns of participation. The patterns are then linked into relationships and structures. Meaning is derived from the participant's relationships and structures.

Qualitative Methods

Research Participants

In order to identify and secure participants for this research, assistance was elicited from individuals within the local Muslim community and email requests were sent to the Muslim Students Association at Binghamton University informing students about my academic endeavors and seeking their assistance with identifying Muslim students attending local public schools who also wore hijab. This process was ineffective and eventually I determined that personal contact with acquaintances and friends regarding finding possible muhajabat participants would be more advantageous because of the poor response received from the email requests and I eventually received commitments from six females to participate:

1 African American / high school student
1 East Indian American / high school student
1 Bi-Racial American (who calls herself African American) / high school student
1 Somali American / high school student
1 Egyptian American / former high school student and current college muhajaba
1 Pakistani American / former high school student and current college muhajaba

The Somali American student moved to Maine directly after our first interview and I was unable to remain in contact with her. The Egyptian American student decided not to participate after our initial meeting but did agree to have a general discussion regarding her public school experiences. The Pakistani American student terminated contact with no explanation. She ended email correspondence and did not return my telephone calls. These changes resulted in my focusing on the three muhajabat students from New York who remained from my original participant list.

Subsequently, I was able to secure three additional participants in the state of North Carolina. I attended several social programs in North

Carolina at a local Muslim organization. After meeting several people on a continuous basis, I was able to discuss my research and secure three additional participants for this study. The first student is going to begin her senior year in high school. The second is a freshman in college and the third is a college sophomore.

Amina, Kamillah, Sumaiya, Asma, Saadia and Reem (pseudonyms) are the six females whom I interviewed to learn more about the experiences of muhajabat attending public schools. When I began interviewing them, Amina was fifteen years old, Kamillah was fourteen years old, Sumaiya was fifteen years old, Asma was seventeen years old, Saadia was eighteen years old and Reem was twenty. These females had commonalities and differences, but they are all muhajabat. The following are charts pertinent to these muhajabat students.

Table 1

Participant Background Information

	Beg. Age	Race	Parents	Parents Religion	Siblings
Amina	15	East Indian	Mother Living	Muslim	Brothers & Sisters
		East Indian	Father Deceased	Muslim	
Kamillah	14	White	Mother Living	Christian	Brothers & Sisters
		African American	Father Deceased	Muslim	
Sumaiya	15	African American	Mother Living	Muslim	Brothers & Sisters
		African American	Father Living	Muslim	
Asma	17	Malaysian American	Mother Living	Muslim	Brothers
		Malaysian American	Father Living	Muslim	
Saadia	18	East Indian American	Mother Living	Muslim	Sister
		East Indian American	Father Living		
Reem	20	East Indian American	Mother Living	Muslim	Sister
		East Indian American	Father Living	Muslim	

Table 2

Participants' School Information

	Education	Current School	Style of Dress in School	Style of Dress Outside of School
Amina	Public & Muslim School	Public 12th	Western with Hijab	Muslim with Hijab
Kamillah	Public & Muslim School	Private 11th	Muslim with Hijab	Muslim with Hijab
Sumaiya	Public & Muslim School	Public College Freshman	Muslim with Hijab	Muslim with Hijab
Asma	Public & Muslim	Public 12th	Western with Hijab	Western with Hijab
Saadia	Public School	Public College Sophomore	Western with Hijab	Western with Hijab
Reem	Public School	Public College Junior	Western with Hijab	Western with Hijab

Data Collection Methods & Analysis

Information gathering for this research occured primarily through interviewing, observations and surveys. The purpose of the interviews was to:

1) Elicit information from the muhajabat regarding their school and social experiences;
2) Probe the muhajabat about their feelings regarding the public and public education experience.
3) Provide an opportunity for clarification of information shared;
4) Grant an opportunity to clarify data that had already been collected.

Observations consisted of watching and recording characteristics and situations that I directly observed. Observations were an important source of data because they allowed me to view the muhajabat in settings that were natural. I always attempted to remain unobtrusive so the muhajabat would not react by changing or altering their behavior. I used surveys to gather further information pertaining to muhajabat attending public schools.

I documented notes of my personal thoughts when observing an interaction or hearing a comment that piqued my interest enough to warrant further thought at a later date. I documented my own reactions to field experiences by keeping notes about anything I deemed peculiar, odd or interesting and that might not be verbalized between the person being interviewed and myself. The research was strengthened when my role as researcher was as definitive and explicit as possible. Taking time to ensure this allowed me to focus on observations without other thoughts being a distraction. Interviews were the primary source of information, and photographs and surveys were further attachments. Integral to the success of this research was my growth as a researcher during the data collection process.

The research process included a reflexive quality of continuous self-awareness. This required patience and genuine commitment to the research topic because it was not necessarily an easy task. Reflexive research acknowledges that the researcher, to some extent, is inseparable from the research topic. Mason (1996) argued, "This means that the researcher should constantly take stock of their actions and their role in the research process, and subject these to the same critical scrutiny as the rest of their 'data' ". (6) A component of research being deemed valid is the researcher's honesty about their role.

I began my research by identifying muhajabat who would agree to being interviewed. Having the opportunity to question and re-question allowed greater and more in-depth information to be elicited. Open-ended interviews of this kind allowed for further exploration of the topic. Schensul and LeCompte (1999) wrote that in this type of interview, "The interviewer is open to any and all relevant responses. There are no correct answers, and the interviewee is not asked to select from a series of alternative choices". (p. 121) The responses are totally up to the discretion of the person being interviewed. It is then up to the interviewer to focus in on pertinent information provided and to develop additional questions, to further knowledge about the person being interviewed in relation to the research question. Being able to listen to information and immediately redevelop a question to gain further information requires skill.

One difficulty was ensuring that the meaning of the phenomena under observation was understood clearly by the interviewer. I remain continuously conscious of the fact that I am a muhajaba. This fostered in me the attentiveness necessary to accurately convey the feelings of the muhajaba I interviewed. My experiences are not relevant while I am eliciting or gathering information during interviews. It is very important that the intended meaning of the people I interview are transferred on to paper without my own experiences or understandings clouding their views. Because of this fact, initially I was concerned when beginning the research process of collecting and analyzing data about muhajabat adolescents attending public schools. According to Rice & Ezzy (1999), qualitative researchers are influenced by pre-existing theory and understandings about their research project: "Our contention is that the most useful response is to embrace it, rather than avoid it. This is best done through being explicit about the influence, right from the beginning of the project". (p. 213) Remaining cognizant of the fact that I am a muhajaba is important, but my concerns regarding being a muhajaba interviewing other muhajabat were dispelled early in the research process.

The experiences of these muhajabat are alien to me. I did not attend a public or public school environment until I was in college. I can only assume or contemplate about what I believe I would have done in their position. Although there may be similarities between their experiences as muhajabat high school students and my adult college experiences, I was unable to tell their story accurately without focusing on the data collected and subsequently analyzed.

Interviews

When researching proven ways to successfully interview adolescents, Ryen (2002) stated, "The interviewer's ability to develop trust and rapport and establish relationships with interviewees facilitates valid data collection". (p. 337) Maintaining good relationships with the research participants was essential to gaining their trust and respect. While these relationships were being established, I also had to acknowledge that even with secured social communications with the muhajabat there were other possible problems that could emerge that had to be recognized. "Power dynamics occur in all interview studies, in that the researcher has control over the research process as well as over much of the interview by virtue of being the one posing the questions". (Eder & Fingerson 2002, p. 183) In lieu of these findings, I also had to focus on how the muhajabat perceived me in the role of researcher while making them as comfortable as possible with the entire process.

The participants always chose the date and time of the interviews. I asked them to plan at least a one-hour block of time for these meetings. After establishing a formal meeting with the persons being interviewed and being granted permission to meet with them, I allowed them to choose a location for their interviews. The actual interviews lasted between forty minutes and one and a half hours. If the participants were noticeably at ease and offering information readily, the interviews lasted over one hour. Whenever I noticed a participant fidgeting or looking at her watch, I would conclude the interview shortly thereafter. This decision was made because I did not want the participants to feel that our meetings were a chore or hardship. These interviews took place over the course of eighteen months.

Table 3

Number of Interviews per Research Participant

Name	Number of Interviews
Amina	Eight
Kamillah	Five
Sumaiya	Seven
Asma	Five
Saadia	Six
Reem	Five

Beginning with comfortable surroundings assisted in collecting information from these females. Using a small tape recorder to record the conversations was beneficial. It allowed me to speak comfortably and use gestures and body language without worrying about taking notes. As long as the participants chose to share or discuss any issue there was time available to do so. However, there were also times when the focus was primarily on taking notes so that I would have the opportunity to write down information a participant emphasized or focused upon intently. Listening to the recordings does not provide these types of particular details or nuances that I can observe visually.

Direct Observation

Gall, Gall & Borg (1999) define direct observation as "The collection of data while the research participants are engaged in some form of behavior or while an event is occurring". (p. 527) Observing individuals while they engaged in an educational setting, or while some event was occurring provided relevant information unobtainable through interviews. These include, for example, having observed

Sumaiya at the library working with another student on a school project or Kamillah and Amina at a pre-wedding and wedding event.[1] In addition, direct observation also lended itself to the development of new interview questions and provided insight about the person's feelings and experiences.

It is important to note that, "One of the core purposes of direct observation is to interpret knowledge derived from what has been noticed". (Rock, 1999, p. 6) I was able to do this after observing the muhajabat in various social settings including home, school, restaurants, weddings and other social events. These observations took place between the fall of 2005 and 2006 & between May and July of 2007. In September through December of 2005, I was able to observe the participants in multiple environments. While I observed Kamillah in school, at home and at a wedding, my observations of Sumaiya took place in her mother's home, her father's home, in school and on outings with her friends. I did attend a pre-wedding party where Amina was present. This was my very first observation of her and I subsequently observed her at a restaurant, at school and with friends. My observations are central to the interviews because they led to some of the questions that I posed to the participants. Asma and I met through her mother, who teaches at a Muslim school in North Carolina. I made visits to the school on several occasions and was introduced to Saadia by Asma who thought she might be able to participate with the muhajabat research. After meeting with Saadia formally, she introduced me to her older sister Reem who also agreed to participate. During direct observation, my analysis as researcher and interpretation of the data were central. Reflexivity is something I gave much thought to once I began consciously critiquing my writing. Making use of mental notes while observing was a reminder to focus on the reality of the person's I am interviewing as I see it, not as I believe it to be. This was an important factor.

Photographs

An extension of direct observation included the use of photographs. Using photographs were uniquely important to this research because

---

[1]   Further details regarding observations are found in chapter five.

they represented a tangible example of the people this work was about. Akeret (2000) expounded on this when he said,

> By looking at photos with a critical eye and a fluid imagination, we see stories emerging: stories about the complexities of relationships; stories about personal quirks and desires; stories about how life changes and how it remains the same; stories about how time and place shape our lives (p. 13).

An issue continuously evolving in conversation when discussing the experiences of females that wear hijab, has been people seeing it as a non-issue. 'It's not like there are lots of muhajabat.

'Do many of them go to school?' I seek to raise the level of awareness to the point that these statements or questions rarely occur.

Utilizing photographs in this research arose after someone asked me, "What is a muhajaba?" Having to answer this question repeatedly, I had an epiphany that providing visual depictions of muhajabat might be an important and necessary component of this research. Photographs of muhajabat might provide an opportunity for people to view them as they are: American students, people attending school, on the phone, every day members of society.

Walker (1999) endeavored to discover how photographs could benefit the research process. In *Finding a Silent Voice for the Researcher: Using Photographs in Evaluation and Research*, Walker (1999) stated, "In using photographs that potential exists, however elsusive the achievement, to find ways of thinking about social life that escape the traps set by language". (1999, p. 37). This salient point is relevant to the muhajabat experience for several reasons:

1) Muhajabat are a relatively new subject in social science research;
2) When Muslim females and muhajabat are the object of discussion in American society, it usually conjures thoughts of oppressed females shrouded in black, which is an incorrect characterization of Muslim females and muhajabat.

Language, to some extent, limits research by requiring the researcher to accept information gathered from interviews, questionnaires and conversations without close scrutiny of what is not verbally shared. Perhaps this is what Walker (1999) meant when he states, "Inevitably, our research is always limited by what it takes for granted". (p. 38) In order to combat this limitation in this muhajabat research, I sought to utilize photographs in addition to the written information collected to assist in educating people unfamiliar with muhajabat and their experiences.

However, although they were still used, the photographs did not remain a key component of the research. This decision was made after I became aware that some individuals viewing the photographs assumed that the races of the females depicted was somehow relevant. Actually, they were merely visual representations for the purpose of illustrating what a muhajaba may look like.

Surveys

Survey I

The opportunity presented itself to ask from four female Muslim school principals and assistant principals the following questions. My purpose was to see if their responses would be similar to one another based upon their commonalities; female, Muslim, muhajabat or if they would vary in relation to other categories such as culture or ethnic origin. The survey was as follows:

Name:
Age:
How long have you been Muslim? Do you have children?
If so, do they attend a public or private Muslim school? Why?
Do you believe Muslim children should attend public schools? Why or why not?
Are there any questions, concerns, or personal information that you could share pertaining to Muslim females who observe hijab and attend public schools?

Even with a sample of four participants, answers varied from one end of the spectrum (Muslims should not attend public school) to the other (after Muslim children learn about being Muslim they can attend a public school). The responses to these questions demonstrate the diversity of Muslim thought and female experiences and opinions as regard education. I specifically asked female, Muslim muhajabat principals these questions to see if this unique, category of muhajabat view public and private Muslim education in the same way with regard to Muslim children and muhajabat.

Survey II

I attended a Muslim social service program conference in South Carolina in November 2005. Muslim women of various socio-economic and ethnic backgrounds were in attendance. I had an opportunity to introduce myself and share information about my doctoral research. Thereafter, I was able to ask anyone who may have had an interest to complete a survey, at which time some did provide their names, email addresses, and contact phone numbers along with their responses. I received twelve completed surveys.

After reading the survey responses, I contrasted the information with some of the experiences of the muhajabat participant interviews and the research regarding muhajabat. There were several commonalities such as an experience referred to by Kahf (2006), who retold her experience of having her hijab snatched from her head by a student. This same experience was reported by respondent nine (Survey II), which demonstrated similar experiences for muhajabat irrespective of race and location. In addition, one of the survey participants suggested using pictures and advertisements of muhajabat to make others more aware of their presence. This was one of my initial reasons for using photographs in this research. Also, these surveys allow for further introspection and analysis of the public school experience for muhajabat. The following is the survey format and questions.

Age:
State:
What is your nationality?
How long have you been Muslim?
How long have you been wearing hijab?
Did you attend public or private school?
Did you wear hijab while in attendance at school? What were your
    experiences like?

How did you feel about being a muhajaba in school (elementary, high school, college)? Do you believe Muslim children should attend public schools? Why or why not?

Are there specific issues that muhajabat face when they are in a non-Muslim environment? What can educators do to provide muhajabat with a positive school experience?

This chapter focused on the advantages of qualitative research as a tool for acquiring meaningful communication and reception of knowledge from the participants that are the focal point of this research. In it, I also shared how data collection and analysis can assist in providing specific guidelines as to how this research can be conducted. The following chapter, "Muhajabat Sentiments", offers a first hand understanding of what some muhajabat experience when attending public schools. An introduction to the six muhajabat that participated in this research is provided in conjunction with their backgrounds and school experiences.

CHAPTER IV

MUHAJABAT SENTIMENTS

The six females I interviewed for this research were all born and raised Muslim, however, their dissimilarities hail from their cultural backgrounds. Their commonality is inherent in the fact that that they are all American. Three of the muhajabat currently reside in upstate New York, and the additional three reside in North Carolina. All six of these females can be described as *Sunni* (Those who follow the path of the Prophet) Muslims although I do not easily ascribe to the use of such labeling because it groups numerous Muslims together whose Muslim beliefs may not be synonymous with regard to hijab. For example, some *Sunni Muslims* may believe that females should only wear dark, somber colors and others may believe clothing color is a personal preference.

Significant to this research (briefly mentioned in a previous chapter) is my role as researcher and my ability to allow the participants to express their experiences without unnecessary interjection on my part. Khan (2000) stated, "While my primary aim was to let the women speak for themselves, there were also times when I interjected or clarified". (p. 26) This statement is comparable to this research research experience where I found it necessary to clarify or restate the participant's verbalizations to ensure their meaning was understood. This method is used, primarily, to safeguard my position as a researcher who has a vested interest in the research topic. I utilized this method most frequently with the three youngest participants. Being objective and not subjective took a conscious effort on my part because the goal was not to influence the muhajabat narratives or entwine my own muhajaba experiences and views with the participants.

During the interview process, a pattern that was evident amongst some of the participants was the literal way they answered questions that I posed. This was true for the participants residing in New York. They were very tentative and seemed to want to express an answer to my specific question without offering an ample amount of additional information. Eder & Fingerson's (2002) words regarding interviewing adolescents became pertinent to me at this time. They stated, "The interviewer should be less concerned with getting his or her questions answered than with understanding the people being interviewed". (p. 184) This statement served as a reminder that I should focus not only on what these muhajabat said but also on what they did not say. Body language, moods, conversation and inferencing also had to be taken into consideration during the interview process. As the interviewing process matured, the participants became less constrained in sharing information about their experiences.

In contrast, the three muhajabat residing in North Carolina began the interviews in a direct, frank manner. I believe that this may have had to do with the age difference between the northern and southern students at the time the interviews took place. Maturity and social development are definitely factors because they are dependent on how females who wear hijab respond to their education and social experiences. I define these as:

1. Maturity and / or having achieved a certain level of growth and development;
2. Social development and associations are components of the responses and feedback that I received.

The average age of the muhajabat in New York was fifteen years at the beginning of the interview process, while the average age for the muhajabat in North Carolina was nineteen years.

Muhajabat Discourses

Prior to discussing participant discourses, it is necessary to provide a definition of discourse as it applies to this research. 'Discourse' is not to be used interchangeably with 'grammar'. Du Bois (2003) explained, "Grammar describes sentences; discourse goes beyond the sentence. Grammar limits options by rule; discourse is what speakers do with the freedom that is left". (p. 47) This means that discourse is what the speaker is offering the listener. The speaker's desire to share, communicate and/or provide information unpredictably is fundamental to the listener being able to derive an understanding of what is being said.

The muhajabat discourses regarding their public and public school experiences as American Muslims that are contained in this research are a result of social relationships between the interviewer and participants that consisted of various expository narratives such as descriptions, explanations and questioning. These discourses were the verbal exchange, conversation and formal discussion that allowed for productive interviewing between the muhajabat and myself.

Amina

I first met Amina at a ladies wedding gathering in April of 2005. Amina and two of her sisters were decorating guests' hands and feet with henna. I began talking to Amina informally about where she studied henna design and about her schooling. I expressed my interest in possibly interviewing her for the research research I was conducting. Amina gave me her number and granted permission to be contacted. A few weeks later I spoke with her brother to seek consent to formally interview her, which he granted. Amina's brother oversees their family business and out of respect and etiquette it is best to seek acceptance from responsible family 104 members before conducting any form of business if one is not a personal family friend or related to the family. Otherwise, trying to gain access for personal contact and conversation would be virtually impossible.

Amina is now eighteen years old. She was born and raised in North India, where she attended a private Muslim school. Amina shared with me how much she enjoyed school in India, which she attributes to having "so many friends." Amina says she wore shalwar (loose fitting pants) and khamees (knee length blouses) along with her hijab and that hijab was a required part of the school uniform. She now resides here in the United States and has lived in upstate New York for the past few years. Amina moved to this country with her mother, brother, and sisters along with other members of her extended family. She is currently completing the twelfth grade at a local high school.

For our first formal interview, I met Amina at her family's restaurant. We sat alone at a back table. I arrived first and chose the setting that would afford us the most privacy. When Amina entered, she smiled and greeted me with 'As Salamu Alaykum (Peace Be Upon You)'. I noticed her tan hijab immediately because it had a snap for fastening under the neck, but she had it unsnapped and thrown over one shoulder instead. She wore a multi-colored loose fitting knee length top with green pants. I began by going over the consent statement and again expressing to her my purpose for completing the research. I asked Amina if she had any questions before we began and she said no.

Casual conversation ensued and I commenced by asking Amina about her hobbies and about school. As the conversation progressed, I made a mental note about how Amina's first year of public school seemed filled with innocence and ignorance of Western school culture.

Throughout the conversation, she demonstrated little awareness of public school culture i.e. adolescent cliques, peer group distinctions (nerds, athletes, etc.) and other dynamics found in public school forums. When pointedly asked about her school day, she happily informed me that she was taking English as a second language courses twice per day and that it was a requirement as well as an easy waste of time. Amina did not volunteer information, but rather waited for me to ask a question or to provide a specific topic for discussion.

In an effort not to stress any explicit subject, I moved the conversation from her current school experience to previous school experiences. Amina shared that she did not attend school with non-Muslims in India. Her knowledge pertaining to non-Muslims in her country of origin is minimal. She referred to non-Muslims as Hindus who "pray to something else." When I asked her about how she felt about attending school with non-Muslims here in the United States, she simply shrugged and smiled. It does not bother her or make her uncomfortable, in her opinion.

Not long after our first interview on a warm Thursday late afternoon, I observed Amina walking towards her home after school. She wore fitted blue jeans, a long sleeve cotton knit blue shirt that ended mid hip and a black hijab. She was walking alongside an Asian female (perhaps similar in age) that also wore blue jeans and a white shirt. She had her black hair pulled back into a ponytail. They chatted as they walked behind the building that led to the entrance of Amina's home.

I saw Amina again the following Saturday when I purchased goods from a sidewalk vendor. She had walked past a grocery store with her mother and sister. She wore a green printed traditional style Indo/Pak suit, loose fitting pants (shalwar) and a knee length blouse (khamees) with slits up to the lower hips on both sides. Amina's mother and sister were both dressed in the same fashion except Amina and her sister wore a hijab and their mother had on a tan chaddah (Usually decorative fabric worn over a female's clothing. It rests on the head and is draped over one shoulder). Amina and I had another meeting scheduled for the following day.

During our previous interview Amina expressed that being a muhajabat is not a problem for her. When I met with her again for our next interview, I explored issues of Muslim dress and dress in the context of school, because of the drastic difference (khamees top that is loose fitting and ends below the knee) in her attire when out with her family or in an Muslim environment, in contrast to the clothing she wears to school (a fitted shirt that ends mid-hip). I hope to further examine her feelings about her identity and how it is related to her dress.

As interviewing Amina became routine, her comfort level increased and she began to share information somewhat more freely in contrast to our first meeting. We discussed her being a Muslim attending public school. She seemed indifferent to the fact that she is a minority at her school. She does not believe that her religion is an issue as a public school student. She said that she could only remember one student even asking her about her religion. A Ukranian student in her ESL class asked her, "Why do you call God Allah"? She said that no one else seemed to take an interest or inquired about her beliefs. Regarding her hijab, Amina expressed that she was comfortable wearing it: "I started when I was like four or five years old." She was living in India at this time. Currently in her first year of attendance at a public school, Amina conveyed that no one inquired about her hijab except a teacher who once asked her if she wore hijab because of a religious requirement. She replied in the affirmative and the conversation went no further. Amina answered questions throughout our conversation without pretense and sometimes responded after some verbal coaxing. I aspired to have continuous conversations with Amina and hoped that they would be increasingly fluid in contrast to direct question-answer sessions.

After several months, I began meeting with Amina again. Frequent smiles and increased conversation describe Amina this academic year. She said the changes in her educational experiences stemmed from heightened comfort with her school environment. "This year, like, people don't talk to me that much about my religion." This statement piqued my interest because during the previous school year she mentioned only one instance when a teacher and a student asked her about her religion or hijab. I deduced from Amina's words that what she really meant was that she was comfortable when she was not made to feel alien within her school environment. Being able to identify with the student population without standing out is equivalent to comfortable for Amina.

Identity is an integral part of the muhajabat public school experience. Roald (2000) stated,

> Identity might comprise the whole gamut of psychological, spiritual and material influences. At certain times or places particular issues are at stake which crystallize around the question of identity. Current controversies involve questions of ethnicity, gender, sexuality and religion. (p. 12)

Being a Muslim muhajaba in attendance at a public school demonstrates how religion is usually an issue that surrounds identity when a female is veiled:

> For Muslim women the issue of multiple worlds is more pronounced than it is for men because of the issue of dress and visibility. Dress, whether one identifies with it as an issue or not, has a subconsciously powerful impact. (Hermansen, 1991, p. 193)

This reality is brought forth in Amina's case through analysis of her own words. Comfort in the school environment is negotiated by remaining obscure. Conversations or questions surrounding the Muslim faith or hijab are not verbalized.

Kamillah

Kamillah, another muhajaba participant, expressed difficulties she faced due to her appearance. Although Kamillah wore regular American style clothing, she also wore hijab and expressed hardship attending public school once she became a sixth grader. She stated, "Well, it was getting harder because I'm Muslim and stuff. I wore my scarf." Being a muhajaba impacted her academic and social experience and added an additional complication to her already diverse life.

At this time, Kamillah was a fourteen-year old vivacious teenager who was born and raised in upstate New York. She has eleven brothers and sisters, seven of whom were raised Muslim. Her father (now deceased) embraced Islam over twenty years ago. Kamillah lives with her mother who is Christian. Her parents divorced years ago but remained devoted to their children and their upbringing. Her mother did not hinder her father from raising their children as Muslims. While he was alive, Kamillah and six of her other siblings resided with him and visited their mother often.

Kamillah is the daughter of an African American father and a White mother. When asked about her nationality, like some other people of color, she refered to race rather than national origin or birthplace. She responded after I asked her about her nationality and for a description of herself by stating, "My dad is black and my mom is white. I've been Muslim my whole life. My dad was a Muslim". Kamillah, according to her own accounts, is dealing not only with a religious difference within the school environment but a racial one as well.

Kamillah has gone to public school most of her life and is now in attendance at a private Muslim school. I first met Kamillah a few years ago. Her older brother is a good friend of one of my brothers. I had an opportunity to observe Kamillah in a Muslim school environment in January of 2005. Thereafter, I met her mother when she was picking her up from school. I spoke to Kamillah's brother (who acts as her guardian) about my research and my interest in interviewing her. On June 18, 2005 I received an invitation to a barbecue at Kamillah's home, and at this time I was able to conduct my first interview.

Kamillah lives at home with her mother and three of her brothers and her other siblings frequent the household regularly. She is second to the youngest. The interview took place in Kamillah's bedroom. She wore tan jogging pants, a pink shirt, and a multi—colored chaddah (fabric that is worn as a partial body covering draped over the head and thrown over one shoulder). Kamilla sat on her bed while I sat on a chair at the end of her bed. Kamillah's room has a full size bed, dresser, and matching vanity set. Over the bed were curtains made from sheer tan fabric which draped from the center point over the bed and trailed down to the right and left of the headboard. Kamillah appeared to be quite comfortable in her room and she locked the door once I sat down.

Kamillah admitted that she did not always wear her hijab in public school. Whenever she felt uncomfortable or out of place she would remove her hijab. Kamillah stated, "In _____, I was the only Muslim girl in the whole school!" Kamillah talks about the constant encouragement from her mother who promotes her to freely choose what religious beliefs she wants to adhere to. "She [mom] used to tell me if you don't want to wear your scarf then you don't have to, but if you want to wear it then you can." Kamillah affirmed her affinity for her faith and avowed her commitment to being a Muslim female that wears hijab.

When I was in attendance at a Muslim wedding that was held at a rented hall, I was sitting downstairs at a table when I took notice of Kamillah entering. She was wearing a lavender and cream pastel burka with a matching scarf and was looking quite beautiful. Her eyes were thickly lined with kohl and her eyebrows looked perfectly arched. She was smiling and talking with three of her friends. When the young ladies sat at a table, I noticed that they leaned towards one another, obviously having a very interesting teenage conversation.

Later in the evening, Kamillah came over to my table to greet me. I told her how glamorous she looked and she smiled. I asked her if she waxed her brows and she told me she *threads*[2] them herself. Kamillah chatted a bit about the wedding before returning to the table with her friends. During my next interview with Kamillah, I asked her to update me about her current school and social experiences and any opinions or feelings that had changed or developed.

---

[2]   Threading is when strings are used and manipulated with the fingers to remove hairs.

Sumaiya

At the onset of interviews, Sumaiya was a sixteen-year old eleventh grader living with her mother, twelve-year old sister and her two brothers whose ages are fifteen and nine.

Sumaiya visits her father on holidays and weekends. Her parents have been divorced for several years. Both of Sumaiya's parents are Muslim and African American. Sumaiya was born and raised Muslim and has lived in upstate New York her entire life. Her father was born Muslim and her mother converted to Islam in her early twenties. Sumaiya has a sense of quietness about her but appears to be self-assured and is very open in conversation. She attended Muslim school most of her life but is now currently attending a public school. Her father would prefer she attend a Muslim school but does not have full custody of her and her siblings and has had to concede to the present arrangement made by her mother.

The interview with Sumaiya took place at her father's home in the room she sleeps in whenever she is there. Sumaiya invited me in but forewarned me that the room was 'junky'. There are a few clothing items strewn on the floor in front of the closet. The room walls are painted a pale blue and there are white curtains decorating the windows. A twin bed, brown dresser and a pole lamp outfits the room. Sumaiya sat down on the right end of the bed and I took a seat on the left. I set my tape recorder between us. Sumaiya loosened her brown hijab from underneath her neck. I noticed that it matched her jilbab (a dress-like garment worn over one's pants and blouse), which was also brown with gold threading. Sumaiya settled in comfortably in her room and we began to converse pleasantly.

One week after our first interview, I observed Sumaiya while she was walking downtown with her brother. She crossed in front of my vehicle at a red light. They both acknowledged me by waving and I waved back. Sumaiya was wearing a navy blue jilbab and a white scarf. She had a black pocket book hanging from her left shoulder and a plastic CVS bag in her right hand. Sumaiya and her brother continued to walk together and eventually faded from my view. This was an unplanned observation that took place in a natural environment. This observation aroused my interest because I immediately noticed that there were no other people in immediate view that were distinctively Muslim. I observed people in the vicinity staring at Sumaiya and her brother. I could not help but wonder if Sumaiya noticed these stares and if her presence had the same effect on students and teachers at the school she attends.

I made a note at that time that I would discuss with Sumaiya what her understanding of hijab is and what her beliefs are regarding Muslim females observing hijab. I am also curious about whether or not she sees her clothing as an extension of her hijab. Today you will come across many Muslim females (young and old) that wear hijab with everyday Western style clothing such as jeans and fitted short shirts. Sumaiya seemed to be very consistent with her Muslim dress so I am interested in pursuing her thoughts on the matter.

Asma

I was introduced to Asma by her mother whom I met at a Muslim school in North Carolina. I stopped to greet her mother at a local Muslim center and, as I had previously mentioned to Asma's mother my goals and aspirations, she agreed to introduce me to her daughter who may be able to assist me with the muhajabat research.

My first meeting with Asma took place in a youth game and activity room in a Muslim community center. Asma had just turned eighteen years old and was registered at a local public school to complete her last year of high school. She was born in Malaysia and attended a Muslim elementary school there before moving to the United States with her parents and brothers. Asma has been in the North Carolina public school system where she has been in attendance for seven years. She is the only girl in her family.

Asma and I sat on a bench in the game room and I began telling her about myself and the research topic. She responded with, "Wow, that's great! I started wearing hijab in the seventh grade." This immediate response opened the door to a very lengthy and rewarding interview. Asma expressed that in sixth grade there was a muhajaba in her class and that they became immediate friends. This relationship is what gave Asma the additional push to don her own hijab, which she did when she returned to school for seventh grade.

Asma shared that her mother consistently talked to her about her maturing as a young lady and the importance of modesty. However, Asma said she was still reluctant because she did not know how others would react. She stated, "My mother encourages me to wear it. She would have preferred it sooner than later. I began wearing it on and off.

Like, not in school but other places. Then I became comfortable with it and now I can't image going out uncovered. It's, like, weird (giggles)."

I could not help but notice how comfortable Asma appeared talking with me. It was as if she had known me a long time. She stands about 5 feet 4 inches tall and has a very petite, thin frame. She smiled frequently and seemed to be in a state of relaxation. Asma was wearing blue jeans, a black and white flowered print cotton blouse that extended to mid thigh. Her hijab was black with black beaded trim and she wore it loosely pinned underneath her neck. Her outfit was accentuated with a large white bag and black flip flops.

Asma began sharing about her life. I asked her what she liked to do when she was not in school and her answer was shop and spend time with friends. She paused in mid sentence and said "my mom still checks my friends and knows where I am going. She makes sure there are no boys and stuff like that." I asked her how she felt about this and she responded, "She's a good mom." Asma is a wealth of information and provided insight into the experiences of religious and cultural minorities in public school. I was estatic that I was fortunate enough to be able to interview her.

It was a humid Saturday with rain clouds in the sky. Asma was standing in a field at a picnic being sponsored by a local Muslim organization. She wore a white, flaired ankle-length skirt, a long-sleeved white shirt, white hijab and a hip length brown tunic/vest. She was chatting and laughing with two females (who appear to be teenagers). The trio began walking to the building owned by the Muslim center. After speaking to a few people outside, I entered the building and once again noticed Asma with the same young ladies. She greeted me and introduced me to Saadia. She told Saadia about my research and Saadia agreed to participate in the muhajabat research.

Saadia

I began interviewing Saadia immediately after meeting her. She was an eighteen—year old North Carolina resident but informed me she was born in New Jersey. She has only one sibling, an older sister. Saadia shared that her parents were born to Muslim families in India, but "you would never know it." I asked her what this meant because it seemed like an odd statement. Saadia said that you would not know her father's family are Muslims. She said that they drink alcohol, smoke and commit haram (forbidden) acts. They came from a Muslim heritage but they do not practice Islam. However, she does not say that they are not Muslim.

Saadia described herself as a regular American teenager who is proud to be Muslim. Her father is a computer programmer for a prominent bank in North Carolina, as well as a real estate agent. Her mother is currently a homemaker, although she volunteers at a local Muslim center to assist with programs when available. Saadia described her parents as Muslims who "discovered Islam" through their children. She said that her parents re-examined their inherited religion and culture after their daughters had begun wearing hijab.

Saadia attended public school her entire life. She and her sister were the only Muslims in the school and it was difficult but she said they persevered. At eleven years of age and in the sixth grade, Saadia said she donned hijab of her own accord. This was a decision she felt was absolutely necessary as a Muslim and was also a turning point in her family's life as Muslims. Saadia's father was against she and her sister wearing hijab. He told them they would face problems and difficulties that he did not want them to have to face. Nonetheless, they did what they felt was right. Saadia said that the first day she and her sister wore hijab, their mother picked them up from school and they were shocked. She (their mother) was wearing hijab and she had not done so before. Saadia said she asked her why and that her mother responded, "What kind of mother would I be if my daughters practice their faith and I did not." They (Saadia, her mother and sister) have worn hijab in public ever since.

Saadia is an average height eighteen-year old young lady with a medium frame. She wore a white hijab pinned under her neck with the ends thrown over her shoulders. Saadia had on a long sleeve white cotton shirt with a large green short sleeve t-shirt over it. She has on loose fitting jeans and sneakers. I began observing Saadia, making note of her expressions, body language and actions. She was accompanying her twenty year old sister Reem who wore an outfit that consisted of an ankle length white cotton sundress, white hijab and long sleeve blue jacket. Reem is several inches taller than Saadia and has a thin frame.

Saadia and Reem are both talking to other young ladies at the Muslim community picnic. They both appear to be enjoying themselves. After several minutes, Asma walks over to the group and begins talking and laughing. They then walked over to the food table to get something to eat.

Reem

Reem was raised in North Carolina and attended public school her entire life. She is currently a student at the local university majoring in Economics and Art History. Reem is twenty years old and is Saadia's older sister. She informed me in our first conversation, "I am proud to be Muslim." She expresses love and commitment to her religious beliefs and way of life.

Reem said she began wearing hijab at twelve years of age and had informed her school friends (all non-Muslims) that she would be doing so. She said that all was well being a muhajaba in the North Carolina public school system until her family moved to a new home and she began attending a new middle school. "Saadia and I were the only Muslims in the entire school." She said, "Eventually people [students] learned more about me and things got better in seventh grade. But in eighth grade, September 11th happened. People in school began to ask me a lot of questions." Reem shares that things changed for her in school. She and her sister were already the only Muslims and the school only consisted of six other minorities who were African Americans. Although they were not the only minorities, she said it sometimes felt like they were.

Reem completed high school and is currently a student at the local university, majoring in Art History. She studied abroad this past semester in London and was very excited about her travel experience. Reem said that she was taking economics and art history classes while in London and that she had participated in several trips and sight—seeing excursions.

All of the research participants provided an inside view to the experiences of muhajabat in public and public schools in the United States. I conclude this chapter after presenting background and observation information about the muhajabat regarding their experiences and the documents of recordings and notes. The following chapter consists of various themes that emerged during the course of interviews/discourses.

CHAPTER V

MUHAJABAT EMERGENT THEMES

During interviews the females express beliefs and share experiences regarding being muhajabat in public school and dressing according to Muslim tradition. Concerning why Muslim females wear hijab, two out of the six females I interviewed had comparatively different answers. Amina states that, "If you are a Muslim you are supposed to wear it. And in Qur'an it says you should wear it and cover your hair." Sumaiya's response parallels Amina's and she also stated that Muslim females are suppose to wear hijab. Kamillah declares that, "We wear it (hijab) for modesty and mostly, basically, it is like a protection, and to let people know that you are a Muslim." The first answer is theological while the others are social.

Saadia answers this question facetiously with, "Cuz we do what we want." Then, in all seriousness, she adds:

> We wear hijab to protect ourselves from the devil. Evil thoughts may wander in the minds of the most pious people, so when we wear hijab, it conceals our superficial beauty. It is also a sign of modesty. Islam teaches us to be humble and modest. Consequently, people befriend us for who we are, not what we look like.

Asma agrees with Kamillah's response that hijab is worn for modesty, but in addition, she adds a unique extension to that view. Asma states,

"We are not eye candy! My dad always uses the example, if given a choice between wrapped candy and candy that has been opened, which would you choose?" This, perhaps, is an analogy that all people can relate to and it serves as a catalyst for further understanding why some Muslim females wear hijab. Asma also adds that, "A woman's beauty shouldn't be on display for the public to see; unworthy, perverted men."

In contrast, Reem answers the question of why Muslim females wear hijab by offering a different answer in comparison to what was previously offered. She shares that, "It is a protection from people who may wish you harm. It filters out people who want to be your friend. For example, like me for who I am." The answers to this question varied between muhajabat, however, none of the answers can be labeled as wrong because they are all reasons why hijab is worn by some Muslim females. Just as their reasons vary why hijab is worn, so too do their experiences.

Muslim, Muhajabat & Public School Student

I asked all of the muhajabat about their experiences with regard to being a muhajaba while attending a public school. Sumaiya responds by stating, "They've been regular. I mean there has been nothing really bad. No one's ever said anything mean to me or treated me bad because of hijab." However, in a subsequent interview Sumaiya was somewhat contradictory when she informs me that she really does not like some of the students and summarizes it to be a problem with them being immature. She states, "The non-Muslim students are mean." This statement indicates to me that Sumaiya makes no direct correlation between her dress and the treatment she receives from some students. Instead, she generalizes non-Muslims as mean. Sumaiya demonstrates characteristics consistent with the synergetic stage of the Minority Identity Development Model expanded upon in the literature review. Sumaiya seems to accept her identity as a Muslim muhajaba and she negates the negative social experiences that her educational environment produces by having a nonchalant or dismissive attitude.

Kamillah views being a muhajaba in school differently in contrast to Sumaiya because she seems to internalize her experiences. She bluntly informs me that, "I feel, like odd, and stuff. Sometimes people didn't want to be my friend or something because I was a Muslim. Or, I would look at some girls and be, like, I wish I could wear some clothes like that". From Kamillah's verbalizations I gathered that she is not comfortable being a Muslim muhajabat in a non-Muslim environment because she is always cognizant of being different. My belief was further clarified when she said,

When I was in public school, I would think people were talking about me. When I first walked in, they would say 'why does she have that on her head?' and stuff or they would sit there and say things. Like after September 11th someone said,

> 'Oh, don't go bomb a building', and then they would say,
> 'Oh, I'm just playing'.

These types of experiences lead to alienation (Goffman, 1963) and feelings of stigmatization. Kamillah is clearly in the conformity stage (self-deprecating attitude) of the Minority Identity Development Model (Atkinson, Morten & Sue, 1998) and views herself as deficient and lacking in the eyes of the general school population.

Interviewing these muhajabat students allows for further insight into the how and why behind the decisions they make. It is quite interesting to listen to muhajabat rationalize why they alter their appearance in school in order to assimilate into a 'socially acceptable' category without realizing that that is what has occurred. For example, Amina explains to me why her clothing went from Muslim fashion to Western fashion. She declares,

> It's because you, like, know in the beginning when I went to school in my uh traditional dress and uh people, they, like, in a group start looking at me, staring at me and it was, like, so embarrassing. So I thought I should change myself a little and I did. But I did not take off my hijab . . . . It was so embarrassing when people started to look at us and stare at us. It's like you are the only individual in society. You know, like, the only one. It wasn't comfortable.

Amina reverts back to her Muslim clothing once she returns home. I also noted after observing Amina several times on the weekends and during holiday breaks that I observed her wearing only traditional

Muslim clothing. Based on this and Amina's own words, I conclude that she feels alienated and out of place with her traditional dress so much so that it becomes a preoccupation in her educational environment. What is important to mention at this time is that these alienating experiences are not limited to school experiences between Muslim and non—Muslims. They also occur between Muslims. Amina voices discriminatory behavior inflicted upon her by other Muslims who do not wear hijab. She states, "In the beginning, when I still dressed according to my religion, my own cousins didn't talk to me. They didn't want to show up like we belonged together or that we were family. They felt embarrassed". Amina, Sumaiya and Kamillah have all experienced alienation and stigma resulting in a desire to assimilate into the school culture. This is a reality that these females appear to be totally unaware. All of these females share their feelings in their own words, which allows for analysis. Kamillah expresses,

> Like when I went to public school I use to wear those kinds of clothes (tight clothes) because everyone else was wearing it and I wanted to fit in. I didn't feel right being the only Muslim in school. But I didn't want to wear it so I always felt bad when I did. But now I am happy I can wear Muslim clothes without feeling weird.

Comfort in the education environment is important to these muhajabat students so much so that they are willing to alter their physical appearance. Feeling alien within their school environment has an adverse affect upon them. Sumaiya, for example, states that ". . . there are other issues like when people look at you like . . . like they think you are strange. Well, I guess it doesn't bother me. I, like . . . hmm . . . feel proud of myself because I like my hijab."

These muhajabat experience the social difference that Goffman (1963) refers to as a result of bearing a stigma. Due to their religious practices, these females have had to learn how to cope in their school environment resulting in them altering parts of their identities. The altering of their clothing allows for social acceptance, which is a quest of persons living with a stigma. In addition, Goffman's (1967) theory about interaction rituals can be applied. During interaction rituals behaviors are shaped (altering of clothing, negative feelings about being a muhajabat) and a person's feelings are affected, which leads to a new attitude or thought produced through the interaction. As the school social experiences of these muhajabat occurs, so too does the complexity of this issue.

Saadia, Asma and Reem all have in common the fact that they have never worn Muslim style clothing to school. I believe that this has had a significant impact on their school experience because they have not had to deal with being viewed as totally different from the peers they attend school with. Aside from the hijab, they appear relatively similar to other females in their school. This does not negate the reality that hijab has the ability to make one be perceived as different in the public and public school environment.

When I asked about how they feel about being a muhajabat in public school, Saadia responded, "It is amazing! I meet many new people on a daily basis and I have a plethora of opportunities to inform people about this great way of life." Asma says,

> I feel good. At first I was nervous. I didn't like my hijab. I didn't feel pretty, etc. But after listening to lectures and having talks with older girls and women, I understood the real reason behind the hijab. Being a Muslim in public school gives you a chance to do dawah. You can't stay in a private, Muslim school or college forever. You have to get out and face the real world.

Reem concurred with Saadia and Asma's intial responses and shares, "I like it. I make friends faster because curiosity about hijab kills them. I am unique, different from everybody else."

Amina, now currently attending a new school in the city next to the family's restaurant, is increasingly talkative in comparison to when I began interviewing her. She said school is going, "pretty good I guess," but compared to her last school, "I don't feel comfortable being a Muslim here." This statement surprises me because Amina had not previously indicated any concerns about being a Muslim muhajaba attending a public school. She did, however, previously report experiencing discomfort that resulted in her wearing Western or American style clothing with her hijab instead of Muslim clothing while she was in school. I asked her why she did not feel comfortable and she responds that it was because of "the way people act and look at us funny." The 'us' she refers to includes her younger sister who attends school with her.

Amina is now eighteen and in the twelfth grade and has advanced from English as a second language (ESL) classes to regents or advanced levels. Amina continues to share her desire to complete high school and informs me that she currently has a 3.8 average. Nonetheless, she feels very much out of place and uncomfortable in her school environment. Amina believed that she was made to feel uncomfortable because she is a Muslim muhajaba. I ask her if there were any other muhajabat attending the same high school other than she and her sister and she says, "No. And I don't think they ever saw students with hijab before. They give me bad looks." I discussed with her how she feels when this happens and she states, "I don't like it but I won't take off my scarf because of it." Amina mentions that at her current school no one ever asks about her hijab. I suggest to Amina that perhaps her experiences did not necessarily relate to her hijab and ask her about her school attire. Nevertheless, Amina insist that it is the fact that she is a Muslim muhajaba. She shares that in school she still wears, "American clothes and hijab, and I guess with hijab to them (students) I look different." Amina said she wears American clothes with hijab to school although she always dresses in Muslim style clothing when she is not in school. I ask her about this choice and she informs me that her mother had made this decision because she believes it will allow them to fit into the school environment since the other children dress like that. In an earlier interview, Amina divulged that she felt very uncomfortable in school when she dresses according to Muslim standards. Later on, she states that she and her sisters have told their mother how alienated they feel, which is why she made the decision she did. This is an understandable effort on her mother's part that did not yield the intended results, which was for her daughters to be able to assimilate via their clothing and in turn feel as if they were accepted members of the public community.

Sixteen-year old Kamillah is still bubbly and displays excitement whenever she speaks. She continues to attend a private school program with twelve other muhajabat students and is in the eleventh grade. Kamillah said, "School is going good right now. I'm comfortable in school and it seems better outside of school. Everyone seems more accepting maybe because there are more Muslims in _____ now." Kamillah continues to wear hijab whenever she is outside of her home. She wears a jilbab/burka sometimes or pants and a knee length blouse. Kamillah says she remembered those times when she attended a public school and, "didn't veil because I wanted to fit in and I was uncomfortable. If I went now I probably wouldn't care what they think but then it was too much as a Muslim." She has grown emotionally and religiously and her growth has assisted her in becoming comfortable with her identity as a Muslim.

During my interview, Kamillah excitedly shares a story that took place at a city bus stop on the north side of town.

> When I was waiting at the CVS for the bus, a guy came over to me and said, 'Are you from Iran'? I said no, I'm from right here. I was born in _____. He was like, why do you wear that? He was talking about my hijab. I said, 'I wear it for modesty'. He said, 'what's the definition of modesty'? I was like 'duh, it's when you don't flaunt your beauty'. He said 'oh, ok'.

I question Kamillah about how she felt when this stranger spoke to her. She intones that she really did not care. It did not bother her but she thought it 'weird' when he asked if she was Iranian. She laughs and seems entertained in a peculiar way while she was telling the story.

Kamillah's current school experiences are positive and she is now blossoming into a muhajaba comfortable with her appearance, education and identity. In earlier interviews she struggled to find her place as a Muslim muhajaba living within a non-Muslim society.

Amina is eighteen, Kamillah sixteen and Sumaiya is now seventeen. An increase in age has occurred along with transforming self-realization and new experiences for these muhajabat. When I began interviewing Sumaiya, she was a self-assured, confident muhajaba who believed that attending a public school would have no noticeable effects on her as a Muslim. After interviewing Sumaiya during the middle of this school year, it became evident that much had changed. When I asked Sumaiya, currently in twelfth grade at the local high school, how school was going she responds, "I can't wait for it to be over." This is in contrast to some of the earlier interviews where she was always eager to learn and experience new things. When I inquires as to why she desires this school year to come to a close so quickly, she flatly responds, "I'm just bored with it and I don't like the people in my class." Sumaiya was unable or unwilling to give me an explanation regarding why and would only repeat, "I just don't like them" twice more.

During our interview we began to talk about Sumaiya's attire. There were noticeable changes. The previous school year Sumaiya wore a jilbab and hijab every day. This year she does not. As I question her regarding these changes, she became defensive. Her posture stiffened and she let out a sigh. She points out, "Yes, I dress differently this year. I wear skirts and shirts now. I don't wear my jilbab to school anymore." When I ask her what inspired her to make this decision, she responds that, "It's just easier. I don't stand out as much. There are other Muslim girls that wear skirts and shirts." This response was informative because in previous conversations Sumaiya never compared herself to other Muslim girls, especially ones outside of her religious affiliations. This, to me, was a significant change. She verbalized a need to justify her decision-making and this seems to make her uncomfortable. I remind Sumaiya about a conversation we had when she told me that, "I'm happy wearing my Muslim clothes." She smiles in memory and I ask her what has changed. "Well, when I first started it didn't bother me wearing burka and hijab but now it's different. Ummm . . . I don't think I dress inappropriately." I ask her what she meant by that and she says, "I still wear modest clothes, long sleeves, long skirts and shirts past my behind." When I question how her new style of dress makes her feel, she responds with a stoic "fine."

Sumaiya had already informed me that she does not wear a jilbab to school anymore. When I ask her if she wears one outside of school, she answers with a surprising "yes." Why?, I ask. She responds, "Because I feel comfortable outside of school. It seems more appropriate to wear it at the mosque, to the grocery store and when I go out shopping. I wear it everywhere else." I interpret this statement to mean that Sumaiya wears a jilbab wherever she believes she will not be viewed as an object of negativity. Schools are social places where individuals must find people to identify with. Wearing a jilbab and hijab prevents Sumaiya from being able to assimilate within her schools various peer groups.

Sumaiya's clothing alterations extend to her hijab also. She use to wear her hijab wrapped around or pinned underneath her neck, ensuring her neck and upper chest were always concealed. Sumaiya now pins her hijab behind her head and loosely ties its two ends in front of her. She says, "I just thought it was better." I, of course, respond with "why?" Her answer was, "Hmm . . . I just thought I should."

Saadia, a recent high school graduate of the North Carolina public school system, was counting down the days to her college freshman experience. Saadia anticipates that she will face "few, if any" issues being a muhajabat in college. She says, "There will always be that minute percentage of people who try to ruin anything that does not conform with the norm of society." However, Saadia feels that allowing anyone to dictate her life choices was an unthinkable concept. She intends to continue to strive hard and achieve her academic goals. I ask Saadia how she would advise other muhajabat attending public and public institutions. She responds with a smile and a strong voice and states, "Don't shy away, be extra friendly. Although it may be difficult at first, it is truly worth everything in the end." Saadia explains that, "Muslims have to go the extra mile. It is not about right or wrong and is not necessarily a good or bad thing. It is just the way it is so why not embrace the differences and move forward?" Saadia is optimistic about muhajabat in public schools all over the world having positive school experiences and she firmly believes this is possible.

Eighteen-year old Asma is a high school senior registered for several advanced placement classes. Asma is happy that this is her last year of high school and eagerly welcomes graduation. Asma is well adjusted in her school experience and in life. She is the eldest of five children, yet functions relatively without responsibilities that sometimes are associated with being the oldest sibling. Asma has come a long way as a muhajaba in public school. She is optimistic about her final year of high school not being fraught with difficulties concerning wearing hijab.

Reem expresses feelings of contentment being a Muslim muhajaba. She shares that she successfully completed high school as a muhajaba and she intends to do the same as a college student. To Reem, she is as American as they come. She enjoys spending time with family and friends, values a good education, loves shopping and is supportive of community programs for children. Being a muhajaba naturally blends in with the culture of her country as well as with her religious way of life. Reem contends, "Some people will always say or do stupid things. I don't let them ruin things for me."

Reem advises other muhajabat attending public and public institutions to "be who you are. Don't let what anyone says get to you." As Reem excitedly prepares for her overseas travel, she informs me, "I want to experience as much as I can prior to getting married." I assume this means that she is engaged but after further inquiry she informs me she is not. Rather, she has decided to fulfill certain goals in life so that when she does get married she can make her marriage her priority.

The experiences that relate to hijab and the attire these females wear are extensive. Some of the continuous changes, alterations, construction and reconstruction of their identity are demonstrated through their daily experiences. The events undergone while these muhajabat attend public schools are also revealing.

Contextualizing School Experiences

Amina describes her current school experiences with difficulty. We discussed how her relationships with teachers are developing during this academic year. She simply says that her relationships at the school she is currently attending are the same as the teacher relationships she had at the school she attended previously. After asking her what this means, she responds, "They are regular, but in class . . . (A long pause and her words ceased)". I encouraged her to finish sharing her thoughts. After a few seconds she reveals, "Students talk about us to other students and it's not good. They were laughing at me and saying to the girl next to me, 'look what you have to sit next to!'." Amina is openly upset and hurt. She then blurts out,

> It is hard to make friends in (current school). They don't talk to us. They give us a different look than in (previous school). I haven't made not one friend. I don't like it. The classes seem hard but I still have a 97/98 average. That's it, I think.

Attending this public school is having a profound effect on Amina. She is now realizing that discrimination and racism exist and that she is not exempt from these ills. I inquire if she believes that her identity as a muhajaba is at all affected. She answers with a quick, "I think so, but you can ignore people and follow your own self." I was curious to discover whether or not Amina feels that there is something the school administration could do to ease her negative experiences. She shares,

No. I don't think the teachers care. You know in the
beginning of the year the principal announced no covering
the head. We were like 'oh my God!' Are these people going
to try and take our hijabs? We didn't understand, but it
wasn't including if it was your religion. It was for hoods and
stuff. We were so scared.

I don't think the school can do anything.

I ask Amina about her teachers and if anything about Islam or the
hijab was discussed in her classes and she responds that it was not. So I
ask if any teachers at the school she currently attends ever asks her about
hijab and she says, "No, but once a teacher said that a silk scarf looked
good on me." She says that the compliment made her feel, "Pretty good
about being Muslim and wearing my scarf." It was the one positive
experience that Amina acknowledges in regard to her current school.

If there were a Muslim school locally that you could attend, would
you? I pose the question to Amina, she was silent for a moment and then
said, "I don't know. I think that in public school people will get used
to us and it will get better." Amina did not seem to have a preference of
public versus Muslim school, as long as her experiences were welcoming
and comfortable. I ask Amina what advice she would give to other
muhajabat also attending public schools. She replies, "Wear your scarf.
It doesn't make a difference that you wear one." When I beseech her
to explain her words, she responds, "It (hijab) is you. Hmm . . . I don't
know, I don't think of changing myself."

I pose the question to Amina: If you have a daughter, would you
send her to a public school? She expresses that she would, "Only if she
dresses the way I would dress." I ask her why and she responds, "She is
a Muslim. She should be what she is." Amina's experiences this current
school year have awakened and broadened her thought processes. In our
earlier interviews, she seemed to be nonchalant about being different in
comparison to the student majority. That has all changed and appears
to have created an atmosphere where she is now required to maneuver
through multiple emotions, feelings, perceptions and a mirage of other
social occurrences.

For Kamillah, the current school year is a peaceful time. Her
mentionable experiences are all based around what occurs in her life

outside of school. She talks consistently about her mother whenever we spoke. She informs me that, "My mother is still really, really comfortable with us (referring to self and siblings) being Muslim. She reads Qur'an in English now. I think she is thinking about becoming Muslim." After updating me about her family, Kamillah began to converse about a time that she was in a store and someone mentioned something bad about Muslims. They had referred to something that they had seen on the news. Kamillah said that the person listening responds and says, "I know a lot of Muslims. They're not bad people. Some people are good and some are bad." Witnessing this conversation supports Kamillah's belief that the city in which she lives is becoming an increasingly welcoming city for Muslims.

She further points out that it does not mean that some people do not continue to have difficulty as regard their Muslim faith. She mentions that she has a friend that attends a school in a neighboring city (the same school Amina currently attends) and that she is constantly being picked on and mistreated by her peers because she is a convert to Islam. She is a White ninth-grader who does not wear hijab. Nontheless, her conversion has sparked indifference within her school community, according to Kamillah. I ask how the school administration could assist with improving public school experiences for Muslim and muhajabat students and she replies that they could choose Friday or one day during the month for people to come to the school and discuss Islam. She believes that there are positive Muslim role models within the community that would not mind doing so. Kamillah also suggests having halal or kosher [kosher meat is permissible for Muslims to consume if halal is unavailable] foods to serve to the students.

Kamillah and I began speaking about a public education versus an education focus around Islam's culture. She believes Muslim school was the best choice for her because she could be with Muslims. Although, she did concede that public schools have a variety of programs that most Muslim schools cannot afford to offer. When I ask her what advice she could offer to muhajabat attending public schools, she replies, "Don't hang out with the wrong people. If people ask you questions about who you are, try hard to explain. Set an example. If you don't know something, its ok, try and find out." These were excellent responses because they offer simple advice that any individual could comprehend i.e. a muhajaba, Christian, junior high school student, etc. These answers are applicable to everyone. Muhajabat, like all people, need encouragement and understanding.

I ask Kamillah if she would allow her daughter to attend a public school if she had one. She says, Yes and no, because it depends on the public school. Most of the public schools are . . . . like, they have distractions that can put you under peer pressure, especially if you are a girl. Certain things boys can deal with better. As far as Islam I think it is harder for girls because they wear hijab in school and that can be hard. Say . . . A Muslim girl is in school and she has friends. Her friends want to have boyfriends and stuff like that. They wear improper clothes to catch boys, and cursing and loud talking about things happens. Some schools might not have all of that. If they do, I wouldn't let my daughter go because I know. Kamillah is very clear about not wanting a child she may have going through the negative public school experiences and struggles that she has undergone. She appears to firmly believe that if she allows this, the results for her daughter would be disastrous and she would be unable to grow up feeling proud to be a Muslim or muhajaba.

Sumaiya's school experiences are intensely poignant. In conversation she mentions that there are only four muhajabat, including herself, currently enrolled in the school she is attending. She estimates approximately ten or eleven Muslim girls all together. Sumaiya reports a positive school experience when, during the month of Ramadan, her English teacher asked her to speak to the class about its significance to Muslims. She says that she felt good about the experience. In contrast, Sumaiya has negative feelings about her government class:

> I feel uncomfortable because we talk about citizenship and resident aliens and people look at me like I am one. One day the teacher said, I just want to know if anyone in here is a resident alien. He didn't say my name but it was obvious he was waiting for me to respond. I was just ready to go.

Sumaiya has acquired an attitude of defeat that she did not previously display. I ask her about friends and whether or not she has made any new ones and she says that she has. She informs me that they are all Muslim. I ask her if she thinks that her new friends influence some of the changes she has undergone, for example, her attire. She responds, "Well, maybe. There are Muslims from all over the world and everyone dresses differently. As long as you are dressed modestly and covered, there is no specific way." We continue to discuss her schooling and I asked Sumaiya what resulted from her and other Muslim students wanting to start a Muslim Students Association (MSA) at her school last year. She says that only a small number of students seemed committed and that the project was forgotten. Nonetheless, she cites an MSA as being good for the students because she believes it would be, "A way to be around people you have something in common with and it would bring Muslim students closer together."

I pose the same question to Sumaiya that I had previously posed to Amina and Kamillah, which was, "What advice would you give to muhajabat attending public schools"? Sumaiya replies, "Wear your scarf because you believe in it and that won't change. You won't feel pressure to take it off." Her choice to use the word *pressure* seems laden with hidden meaning. I question Sumaiya regarding whether she felt pressured to wear or not to wear her hijab. She responds, "No. I never felt pressured not to wear it or to wear it." What is your response when someone asks you why you wear it? "I say, 'It is part of my religion and my hair is sacred, not something for me to share with everyone'." Sumaiya's religious convictions appeared to be the same in comparison to our earlier interviews. What is recognizably different is the manner in which she seems to be able to live out her convictions and beliefs.

Sumaiya's public school experiences are weighing upon her but she is willing to share only portions of her feelings at this time. In previous interviews she was much more giving and open to sharing who she is. She is a perceptive young lady who seems to be learning how to manipulate the many dimensions of her identity and school experiences. I ask Sumaiya if she would allow her daughter to attend a public school. She says, "I don't have a problem with it, but I'm in public school only because I don't have a Muslim one to go to." This response connotes to me that Sumaiya would mind because of her need to justify why she is attending a public school. This does not indicate intentional criticism on my part but rather recognition that this was a question that the other muhajabat did not answer in a manner that could be construed as defensive.

Asma does not remember having experiences that she could interpret as negative while in school. She does, however, cite an experience during the course of one of our conversations that she describes as a "positive muhajabat experience." Asma states,

> There was a girl in my class and I didn't know that she was Muslim until I found out that she was fasting during Ramadan. After winter break she came to school with hijab on and said that I had inspired her. I felt good.

The public school Asma attends has three other muhajabat in attendance, one African American and two Pakistanis. She said she has never heard of Muslim females having difficulty in school because of their hijab but then added that the other muhajabat are not in any of her classes and she usually only sees them in passing.

Asma imparted that her experiences with students have been similar to her experiences with teachers. That is, both ask questions about her hijab and after answering "I wear it because it is a part of my faith and for modesty," neither usually pursue the questioning any further. Asma believes the administrators and teachers should enforce dress codes to make the school experience comfortable for all students, including muhajabat. She says, "It is kind of uncomfortable when people wear short shorts, showing too much skin. These are the dress issues schools should be worried about." Asma feels that wearing hijab encourages people to look at muhajabat as human beings and that the hijab solicits respect:

> You're not eye candy. Wearing shorts and tank tops and having guys look at you with lust. We don't need that. Guys give respect to muhajaba although people don't tell you that.

I inquire of Asma if she would attend a Muslim school versus public school if given a choice. She responds, "Umm, no. You will have to go out in the open anyway." She does not deem it necessary for muhajabat to attend a Muslim school. Asma then adds, "I imagine teasing, like calling people bald or asking if they have hair, may be experienced by some." I found this comment to be rather peculiar because Asma had informed me that she never had a negative school experience that could relate to her being a muhajabat. I used the opportunity to inquire why she feels such teasing may occur, but she was unable to provide me with an answer.

Surprisingly, when asked 'If you had a daughter would you send her to a Muslim or public school'? Asma informs me that she will send her daughter to a Muslim school first. I asked why and she responds that, "It is what my mom did with me. I turned out pretty good." I responded to her comment with a smile and gave thought to her answer.

On the other hand, Saadia described her sixth grade muhajaba experience as "very hard";

> I didn't know anyone. Students taunted me and made fun of me. I was called names, I got dirty looks and paper balls were thrown at me. But I had a sixth grade social studies teacher and he was very nice to me. He helped me through being a muhajaba.

Saadia said that after surviving sixth grade, seventh was very much improved. According to Saadia, this occurred because she made some friends and became outspoken. "I started to explain my religion." She shares that at least fifty percent of the friends she has today are people who asked her about her hijab when they first met.

Questions regarding hijab were asked by teachers, but Saadia said that she never experienced any negative comments. She points out that, unfortunately, this was not the case with some students and other school staff. I ask her to explain this comment and she describes the following:

> In high school I was on the track running with some of my friends and a girl came and pulled my hijab off. My non-Muslim friends started yelling at her. I didn't really have to say anything.

On another occasion,

> The referee would give me problems at soccer games about wearing long pants and hijab but my coach would stand up for me. Mof of my non Muslim friends stood up for me.

I asked Saadia how she felt when these situations arose and she stated that it bothered her but she was glad to have people defend her.

Saadia relates the school experiences most vivid in her memory,

> It was my senior year. Every two years principals would change at my school. I was wearing hijab and the new principal said "take that off! It is against school policy." I told her it was my religion. All I remember is her arm reaching towards me. A teacher came up behind her and told her, "She can't take it off."

Saadia says she just stood there momentarily. She remembers feeling "something" and says when she thinks about it she still remembers feeling shock as the principal reached towards her but was grateful things did not escalate beyond that.

Saadia also told of another incident that occurred with a principal when she was a junior in high school:

> It was a new male principal. He saw me in the commons and said 'wait here'. Then he came back and walked me to the office. He left the office and came back with a female administrator. They both then took me to a back room. When we were inside they told me I wasn't allowed to have my head covered. I said I wasn't taking it off. They made me write a letter saying it was my religion and made me sign it. Then they told me I could leave.

Saadia said she remembers looking for her sister and telling her what had happened. She believes that the negative experiences related to hijab that she has gone through are all in the past. Saadia relates to them as mere growing pains. She is quite optimistic.

Regarding school administration and muhajabat, Saadia believes that they can assist Muslim students in assimilating to the public and public school environment by providing foods that are acceptable to Muslim dietary standards in school cafeterias and accommodating gym classes by offering an all girls' class. Saadia explains that these efforts would be beneficial to both the students and the school.

Saadia feels that she is moving right along with life despite other people's perceptions of her. She mentions that, "At the mall people stare and everything but we don't care now. In a car people will gawk but it doesn't matter." Saadia is a refereshing example of the human spirit at its best. She does not focus on or become absorbed with past experiences that are negative, uncomfortable or disheartening.

I ask Saadia about school preferences if she were raising a muhajaba and she responds, "I would send my daughter to public school so she could learn how to function in this society." This is a key concern for Saadia because she believes it is imperative for muhajabat to survive and exist within American society as contributing members.

Saadia's sister Reem says her school experiences were literally planned. In fifth grade she made the decision that she would begin wearing hijab. She informed friends so that when she returned to school after summer vacation they would not be shocked when they saw her. Reem feels that from sixth grade through the beginning of eighth grade, her experiences were inconsequential until September 11, 2001. Reem says that after 9/11 students acted the same but began asking many questions. The pinnacle of her public school encounters occurred when, "In science class a female, white teacher said, 'The more Christians they kill the more they go to heaven'. I was so shocked. Reem remembers feeling unsure and angry. She went home and discussed the situation with her mother who in turn shared it at a Parent Teachers Association meeting. The PTA representative spoke with the principal about the school having a teacher that would make such a biased and uneducated remark to students. The principal addressed the issue at a staff meeting.

Reem shares that she and her sister were members of a local Muslim Girls Scout troop. Around the time the above incident occurred, her troop was spending a day with a local newspaper reporter. The reporter participated in activities and conversations with the girls. She asked them about school and Reem shared with her the uncomfortable incident. The reporter decided to write an arictle about the incident and it was published on October 2, 2001 in the Charlotte Observer. Reem believed that this story being printed provided an opportunity for the public to learn about Muslim females in attendance at public schools and important issues they may face.

I ask Reem her overall opinion about public school and what her decision would be regarding sending her own daughter (if she had one) to a public or Muslim school. Reem responds,

> If I had a child I'd want her to go to public school. In my experience I realized that many Muslim school girls are ignorant about some things. We were at an amusement park with Muslim school girls and they didn't know how to act socially. Like, some of them didn't want to get on one of the rides because they didn't want to stand on the line with boys. I mean you can't ask people not to stand in the line. That is what I mean.

Reem concurs with her sister's belief that muhajabat have to learn how to function in this society and that this will not occur if they do not become mainstream members of our society and American culture. This perspective continues to be debated by Muslim educators, politicians, parents and religious leaders.

One of the distinct differences between the muhajabat I interviewed in the south in contrast to those I interviewed in the North is that the Southern muhajabat did not wear or attempt to wear Muslim style clothing to school. I asked Saadia, Asma and Reem if they believed their school experience would have been different if they wore jilbabs or shalwar and khamees to school. Their responses were as follows:

Saadia   Yes. It would differ from my current experiences because I would not have conformed as much to American trends as much as I do wearing western attire. I don't think my experiences would vary significantly, but I think they would be a little different.

Asma   Yes, I think it would've been different. Teenagers these days focus so much on fashion, appearance and clothes. The girls are very materialistic. I'm certain that I would've had a different experience had I worn a jilbab/shalwar and khamees to school I think it would've been harder for the kids in my school to accept me. It would probably need some getting used to.

Reem   I would say that my life experiences would have been different. The reaction of people would have been different, more wary. I would take a guess that my experiences would have been worse.

The responses to this question brings forth an issue raised by some parents and advocates of Muslim schooling. That is, Muslim clothing, including the hijab, plays a significant role in a Muslim's identity. If it is not worn, their identity will be affected.

Saadia, Asma and Reem assimilated into their school environments through dress, with the exception of the hijab. They made a conscious effort to exist within their education and school environments irrespective of the stigma they bore. I believe that because these females were immersed early in public school culture as muhajabat who wore western attire, it was easier for them to survive within the school socially and academically. Clearly these three females are and have been in the synergetic stage of the Minority Identity Development Model. They each accepted the fact that they are muhajabat and are comfortable being such.

Articulation of Goals

One of the education goals that Amina, Kamillah, Sumaiya and Asma have in common is their desire to complete their high school education successfully and attend college. Amina speaks candidly about her express wish to become a doctor. She intends to begin college immediately after she graduates. We spoke about the hard work and dedication necessary to become a doctor as well as the fact that she is a Muslim muhajaba. Amina states, "I don't think that wearing my scarf will be a problem in medical school." She does not believe that` any of the muhajaba experiences she has had during her attendance at public schools has any relevant connection to attending a public college as a muhajaba.

Kamillah also intends to become a doctor. She shares that, "I want to become a pediatrician. Umm . . . I like dealing with children. I don't want to go away to start college though. I think I want to start at the local community college because it's a smaller school and it's where I live right now." When I asked about being a muhajaba in college, Kamillah responds, "It won't matter. I don't think anyone will mind." Kamillah, like Amina, views college as a place where social freedoms abound for each and every student and as a place where stigma and discrimination do not exist.

Sumaiya ponders over the question, 'What would you like to do after you graduate?' When she responded, she states that:

> I am going to go to college and major in international relations. I see a lot of stuff going on in the world and I want to better it, like how our country deals with Muslim countries or countries where a lot of Muslims live. I want to work to help people understand Islam more. That is what I plan to do.

I ask Sumaiya if she feels that she will face any issues as a muhajaba in college and she replies, "Probably some of the same experiences I have had in public school. But that will not stop me. You can't shut yourself off from other people. They will accept who you are eventually."

Sumaiya, in contrast to Amina and Kamillah, observes the public school experience in a manner that allows her to make conclusions as to its relevance to her everyday life. She acknowledges that her feelings of displacement, her attempts at assimilation and her altering of her identity are occurrences that may all have a place in the next phase of her educational career. Because Sumaiya is so astute, I believe she will be successful in completing college. Amina and Kamillah, to me, will probably have great difficulty in college based upon their feelings and experiences that they revealed to me. Their comprehension regarding the social and political climate of their communities and the world at large are limited. They have little understanding about school experiences being possibly transferable between high school and college. Ultimately, I believe that if they were to experience any negative effects to their identity such as they previously experienced in high school, such experiences may set them back emotionally, which can lead to them rethinking their goals of college success.

Regarding the muhajabat in the South, Asma would like to attend Chapel Hill and major in pharmacy after she graduates. Asma concedes that there is probably a fifty-fifty chance of her facing issues in college that relates to being a muhajaba. However, she states that, "I have never really faced any negative issues since I started wearing hijab, but I am sure I'll still get questions and comments." Contrasting Asma's viewpoints with those of Amina and Kamillah, I hope that her college endeavors are free of bias that relate to her being a muhajaba. Otherwise, she will probably be negatively affected because she does not directly relate to the negative educational experiences of muhajabat nor does she seem to realize that one day they could happen to her.

I forsee both Saadia and Reem being successful in every endeavor they make. They are both remarkably resilient and have the determination to accomplish their goals. Saadia will begin double-majoring in International Studies and International Business at the local university and Reem continues majoring in Economics and Art History. Saadia believes she will face few, if any, issues being a muhajaba in college. "There will always be that minute percentage of people who try to ruin anything that does not conform with the 'norm' of this society." Reem says she has not had to cope with negative college experiences related to being a Muslim or muhajabat other than when their local Muslim Student Association office having been vandalized on campus. "Some of our signs were destroyed and things were vandalized." Nonetheless, she said she would continue her studies and travels as she has planned.

Muhajabat receiving suggestions regarding how to succeed when they face unpredictable and/or challenging experiences from one's peers, teachers and families are incentives to continue endeavoring to achieve their school goals. Alienation and stigma can result in these students discontinuing their educational strides while at the same time it can negatively affect their identity. Positive communication and acknowledgment of what some muhajabat face in public schools are necessary for their academic survival.

In concluding this chapter, it is important to mention that during my final interviews with the participants, I asked all of the muhajabat "If you were to describe yourself to someone, what would you say?" The following were their responses:

Amina   I am a polite person that is very religious.

Kamillah   Ummm . . . Probably I'd say that I am independent and
            outgoing. I have patience with people even when they don't
            understand certain things.

Sumaiya   I'm an American Muslim (long pause). I am a Muslim who
             is American. Saadia I would say that I am an open-minded,
             semi-liberal Muslim female.

Asma   That I'm very open-minded and friendly. I try to make
             people around me feel comfortable. I'm very easy to get
             along with.

Reem   That I am just like any other person you would meet on
             the street. I just look different.

After comparing these responses, what I discovered and found
most striking is the fact that none of the muhajabat mention race. A
commonality between Amina, Sumaiya and Saadia is that they all
mention Islam (their religion and way of life) as a component of who
they are. Kamillah obliquely refers to this when she spoke about people
not understanding certain things.

In addition, of the six muhajabat, only two can be placed in the
category of immigrant. Amina lived for several years in India and Asma
left Malaysia as an elementary school student. However, both Amina
and Asma appear to be well-adjusted to American society and neither
of them views themselves as having experiences that differ from their
peers based on their land of origin. In other words, they do not view
themselves as immigrants but rather as Muslim, muhajabat Americans.

These muhajabat discourses articulate the complexities of their
public school experiences. The continuous changes, alterations and
reconstruction of their identity have been demonstrated. In order for
schools to address the challenges and difficulties these muhajabat face,
they must first learn about Muslim muhajabat beliefs and experiences
so that their educational needs may effectively be met. Chapter six
introduces *Hijab Theory* and discusses how multicultural education can
positively impact the education experiences of muhajabat.

CHAPTER VI

PUBLIC SCHOOLS AND MUHAJABAT

In order to comprehensively address the public school experiences of muhajabat, it is necessary to not only have a theoretical approach but to also involve all persons who participate in their education, i.e., administrators, teachers and support staff. Educating principals, teachers and students about a growing population in public schools would benefit not only the muhajabat but also the entire school community as a whole.

Bullock (2002), Haw (1998) and Zine (2006) all discussed the need for an ideology that would address the issues Muslim women and muhajabat face. Bullock (2002) espouses the importance of the nativity or origin of women to dictate the equality that they advocates for and/or received. In contrast, Haw (1998) expresses her commitment to feminism because of her desire to understand "the differences and dominations between and within femaleness and maleness". (p. 30) Additionally, Zine (2006) identifies herself as a Muslim scholar and feminist. Zine believes that feminism can assist in tackling gender Islamophobia, which she defines as "Specific forms of ethno-religious and racialized discrimination leveled at Muslim women that proceed from historically contextualized negative stereotypes that inform individual and systemic forms of oppression" (Zine, 2006: p. 240).

However, these scholars do not provide a delineated description of their beliefs regarding how their ideologies would be applied or what the components of their ideas are. Muhajabat need a framework unique to their experiences. There needs to be consistent recognition and representation of what muhajabat experience and who they are. I came to this conclusion after completing interviews, observations and surveys. These thoughts have encouraged me to develop a theory that could help people broaden their worldview as regards this particular group of people. These thoughts resulted in me coining the term *Hijab Theory*, whose purpose is to explain phenomena and occurrences related to the muhajabat experience.

Hijab Theory is not about new terminology, but rather, naming one's struggle, being empowered enough to share what that struggle is and renaming it according to the experiences of the muhajabat. Bullock (2002) uses the term 'indigenous feminism' to give a name to a new theory that will address the needs of Muslim and Arab feminists advocating for political, social and economic equality for women. What I am suggesting is that an additional step be taken beyond this view towards a new theory: *Hijab Theory*. This theory can be utilized as a cultural broker to explain the hijab framework while providing relevant information pertaining to adolescents that wear hijab.

A female ideology addressing the specific interest and issues of females who wear hijab is necessary to help transform societal misconceptions and ignorance into factual information and tolerance. Muslim females globally are being forced into unrelenting, scrutinized boxes rather than being looked upon as mainstream members of society. A cultural theory grounded in Muslim ideology based on Islam's principles becomes necessary and can be used as an instrument of empowerment to assist muhajabat with becoming visible members of society with voices that are heard.

In addition to inquiring about an ideology beneficial to Muslim females and muhajabat, the viewpoint of Haddad, Smith and Moore (2006) who, as non-Muslims, provide their scholarly analysis of what Muslim feminist discourse means in the context of Muslim communities in the Untied States, discover that,

> What has been labeled Muslim feminist discourse in the West is the result of exposure to and influence by Western liberationist discourse and postmodernist analyses, blended with the recognition that Muslim women face their own circumstances that may not fit with Western feminist models. (pp. 154-155)

Extending the feminist discussion further, another component termed womanism emerged. Womanism essentially can parallel much of the indigenous feminist goal, which was not using Western thought as the ideal for understanding female experience. Ulen (2005) defines herself as a Muslim womanist. However, she does not view feminists as adversaries. Rather, she suggests that, "Any concerted efforts to link and liberate on the part of American feminists must proceed from factual knowledge of the veiled 'other'" (pp. 44-45). Once this is done, Ulen believes feminism, womanism and Islam can be quite compatible.

Although it is possible that we can relate to and understand some of the muhajabat experiences using womanisms theories, womanism still does not capture the essence of being a muhajabat because of the absence of Muslim beliefs and teachings. The official term, *Africana Womanism,* was coined in 1987 by Hudson-Weems. Hudson-Weems explains

> *Africana*, identifies the ethnicity of the woman being considered, and this reference to her ethnicity, establishing her cultural identity, relates directly to her ancestry and land base: Africa. The second part of the term, *Womanism,* recalls Sojourner Truth's powerful impromptu speech "And Ain't I a Woman," one in which she battles with the dominant alienating forces in her life as a struggling Africana woman, questioning the accepted idea of womanhood. (pp. 153-154)

In other words, womanism focuses on the struggles of the African woman while challenging the organized bodies of power that encompasses her world. The seeds of womanism were sown and grown in Africa. Africans have a legacy of living in family-oriented societies that promote a dominant world-view of family being the lifeblood of everything valuable. Nonetheless, African culture is steeped in tradition and in many situations females are seen as subordinate to males. In African societies, gender hierarchies exist but this does not limit or diminish the strength and character of African women and the influence they have in their societies, however unofficial it may be.

African American women also advanced their own concept of womanism. Walker's (1983) term womanist refers to a person who is "committed to the survival and wholeness of an entire people" (p. 155).

A commitment to human beings as one complete existence is what is being referenced. There is no need to separate the needs of males and females, rather the focus lays in effectively discussing how we as a whole can improve the status of women. Nonetheless, Walker's view of womanist is not interchangeable with womanism as Walker's theory is central to the woman's sexuality and culture being at the center, which compares closely with feminism except for minute differences. The needs, desires, struggles and experiences of African females are what African womanism is grounded in, along with African culture.

Womanism (whether the African or African American version) does not allow for women to self-define themselves religiously. Self-definition is an important component of being female, in actuality, being human. Therefore, any group or individual should be able to effectively define their self without feeling devalued by society. The fact is that:

> The image of Muslim women as passive and oppressed has gained currency because it signifies beyond itself to a general category, such as a faith and a culture. In both cases their look is the same: They are more or less exotic, more or less veiled, more or less available, more or less oppressed. This is the image with which they will always have to contend. (Cooke, 2001, p. 130)

These images of Muslim females have to be challenged systematically in order for them to achieve recognition as human beings with the same value and positive attributes that are identified with other groups of females. The development of hijab theory would aid in combating how muhajabat are perceived negatively and promote an informed understanding of them and their religious and social choices in a positive manner.

The proposal of hijab theory, which I believe is necessary in the context of the United States, focuses on two specific categories, irrespective of the fact that there are a multitude of other reasons that some Muslim females may veil.

1. Acceptance and obedience of the Holy Qur'an and Sunnah, which includes the religious injunction that hijab is incumbent and that its role is to preserve modesty and contribute to societal

order. In this role, modest behavior partners with modest dress and piety.

Components of this category include:

- Belief that the Holy Qur'an is the fountainhead and authority for Muslims and that hijab is presented in its content;
- Acknowledging that the teachings of the Prophet Muhammad (PBUH) include veiling for females when they are in public and in the company of males not directly related to them.

2. An expression of religious identity, which becomes important to many muhajabat, especially when they reside in a non-Muslim environment.

Components of this category include:

- Projecting a positive image of Muslim females;
- Encouraging Muslim feminine pride;
- Demanding respect as a person and not being judged or objectified as a female. Some muhajabat believe that men are less likely to objectify them or become verbally and/or physically disrespectful when a female is veiled.

What has emerged in the United States as an increasing problem is the ability of muhajabat to freely express their Muslim identity when it is inclusive of wearing hijab. Opposition, critiques and intolerance towards hijab are springing forth as a major struggle for Muslim females residing in a Judeo-Christian dominant society. Factors leading to this phenomena are linked to the notion that females covering their hair in public are somehow anti—democratic, a tool of male oppression, and that hijab decreases the freedom and mobility of females. These ideas are promoted, in large part, by non-Muslim feminists and politicians who would like to see their own social beliefs as the dominant world-view for everyone, even though claims are continuously made that every individual has the right to choose. Nonetheless, choice does not seem to extend to muhajabat rights to veil in public. Shakeri (2000) expresses that muhajabat,

> Argue that they are wearing hijab out of their own free will. They are content with it and feel liberated. As women, they feel they are true to themselves, a key concept in feminist ideology. To their surprise, however, Western feminist use the same argument Muslim fundamentalists use in the Muslim world, viz., these women should be stopped for their own good. (p. 135)

As Shakeri indicates, muhajabat are not extended the same respect regarding personal choice that other females rightfully possess. It is this type of mentality towards hijab that continues to foster indifference in a society that is already wrought with anti-Muslim tensions. The dominant group's ideology of assimilation and integration seems to be applicable to specific groups, one of which is muhajabat: "Muslims, particularly women, want to keep their religious identity, while adopting the other aspects of the host culture such as language, educational system, employment patterns, and civic life" (Shakeri, 2000, p. 129). The participation in Western and democratic values such as language, education, and integrated employment should suffice to demonstrate that these females appreciate the lifestyle and culture of the society in which they are members. Their style of clothing should not adversely affect their ability to be respected members of society. Education can assist in resolving the conflict about Muslim females observing hijab. Factual information about Muslim beliefs and hijab can be incorporated within our educational and social systems. Schools, businesses, and political forums can help to eradicate the prejudice and discrimination that muhajabat experience: "What must be recognized is that ignorance supports prejudice; accurate information can help to reduce prejudice" (Sleeter & Grant, 1999, p. 92). Through education, a conscious effort can be made to understand the components of hijab theory thereby understanding the complexity and diversity of the muhajabat experience, and hopefully shaping future experiences for the better. Henceforth, an additional key component to hijab theory is multiculturalism. Multiculturalism is a pertinent constituent to hijab theory because it can be used as an extension to hijab theory's goals by encouraging and teaching tolerance of a minority group whose beliefs and identity are on constant display.

Hijab theory is a work in progress that transcends this research. It is a work I intend to develop and promote with the specific purpose of advancing the reality of muhajabat in the social context of our society not only to encourage awareness, but to offer a knowledgeable perspective regarding an issue that is currently having social, ethical, emotional and political implications globally. In conjunction with this long-term goal, it is important to address how improvements in the public education system can be achieved in order for muhajabat attending these institutions to benefit. Issues regarding school policies, curriculum, teachers and administrators are all educational components that need to be scrutinized in the context of the muhajabat student experience.

Public Education and Hijab

In public schools throughout the country, muhajabat face difficult school experiences affecting their faith. Whether the issue is wearing the hijab in gym, changing clothes in the locker room, or the hijab being considered 'unnecessary headgear', the problems are numerous. Becoming educated about the hijab is one way to help dispel misconceptions or stereotypes. Instituting factual information about hijab into the curriculum can help students understand the complexity of this subject.

As a muhajaba, I find it necessary to critique my own beliefs, feelings, and opinions with regard to hijab. I realize that the teachings contained in the Holy Qur'an and Hadiths are not the single motivating factor for every Muslim female who wears hijab, although it is my own. Reasons may range from customs to state laws depending on the country in which the muhajaba originates or resides. By contextualizing the muhajabat experience within the United States and its public schools, it can be surmised that just as the meaning of the hijab may vary among individual muhajaba, so will their reasons for wearing it in the United States. Irrespective of why Muslim females wear hijab, what is of great importance is that the views of non-muhajabat should not be imposed upon them. This has become a serious issue in the United States where hijab is consistently portrayed in the media as an oppressive component of a foreign, heretic religion. As Bullock (2002) states, "The sociological complexity of covering is not captured by the conventional wisdom in the West that holds that the veil (as if there was just one type) is a symbol of women's oppression in Islam". (pp. 86-87) In fact, there are multiple ways of styling the hijab and the many styles muhajabat use may also depend on the ethnic and cultural group to which they belong.

Barron was the first to publish a book that specifically focuses on hijab styles. Her book, entitled *Focus on Scarf Styling* (1994), uses visual demonstrations to describe how to wear various hijab styles and also includes hijab accessories. I spoke with muhajabat who were able to purchase or read this book and they seem pleased with their religious and cultural practice being demonstrated in a positive, colorful and fashionable manner. Wearing the hijab not only allows Muslim females to practice their Muslim beliefs; it also allows Muslim females to maintain their Muslim identity in a free, democratic, Western society whose values offer the opportunity to all to be whomsoever and whatsoever they are. West (1995) states:

> How you construct your identity is predicated on how you construct desire, and how you conceive of death: desire for recognition; quest for visibility; the sense of being acknowledged; a deep desire for association—what Edward Said would call affiliation. It's the longing to belong, a deep visceral need that most linguistically conscious animals who transact with an environment (that's us) participate in. And then there is a profound desire for protection, for security, for safety, for surety. And so, in talking about identity, we have to begin to look at the various ways in which human beings have constructed their desire for recognition, association and protection over time and in space, and always under circumstances not of their own choosing. (pp. 15-16)

Muhajabat, like other human beings, wish to feel safe and secure in their surroundings.

School Administration and Hijab

It is imperative that administrators and principals are educated about Islam and muhajabat. School leadership plays a key role in the muhajabat experience. Teachers cannot be expected to educate students about issues that administrators do not deem important or relevant. With the increase of Muslims in the United States and throughout the world, it stands to reason that there will be at least one muhajaba in many public schools sooner rather than later: "Islam is the fastest growing religion in America and in Europe. There are, for example, more Muslims in America than in Kuwait, Qatar and Libya" (Esposito, 2000, p. 3). Therefore, administrators and principals can prepare themselves through religious and cultural education to accommodate this growing population. Being informed about an issue such as muhajabat in public education prior to having muhajabat in attendance at these schools can only strengthen the social dynamics of the school. Learning from the mistakes or wise decisions of other schools is perhaps the best way to promote diversity and a wholesome education for all students. Seeing that teachers and other school staff receive factual information and training in working with a minority group such as muhajabat would aid in promoting curriculum that correctly addresses the issues related to veiling and the experiences of muhajabat.

Also, stigma and alienation are important in relation to developing social support networks. Principals and schools that support the development of a Muslim Student Association (MSA), as in the case of one of the females interviewed, is a responsible way to start. This is an example of how principals and schools can make a positive difference in the public school experience of muhajabat.

Curriculum and Hijab

Joan Bohorfoush was a social studies teacher from Portland, Oregon. In addition to teaching, she was also a radio producer and social activist. What makes Joan Bohorfoush unique is the memorial curriculum developed after her death from cancer in 1997. *Scarves of Many Colors, Muslim Women and the Veil* was part of the work she committed to for the purpose of bridging cultures. She completed research and interviews to fulfill her curiosity and learn about muhajabat and their every day life. Bohorfoush's curriculum began with an introduction that looks at stereotypes of Muslim women and explained why the context in which people veil or wear hijab matters. The introduction is followed by four lessons that range from the use of photographs for students to explore the differences between themselves and others to studying transcripts of Bohorfoush's interview of a Muslim woman with Bohorfoush's questions edited out. The curriculum ends with resources that may be used for further information pertaining to Muslim females and hijab. This curriculum could be adopted by schools, particularly high schools, so to present the topic of Muslim females wearing hijab. The curriculum provides the differing opinions of various Muslim females, which will help teachers and students alike to understand the great disparity of opinion even amongst Muslims. Although it is a beginning, it should definitely not be accepted as a final work to present the muhajabat experience in classrooms; rather it can be looked upon as a work in progress.

Presentation of the muhajabat experience in the context of where they live and attend school is important. Otherwise, muhajabat can be yet again marginalized by the techniques and presentations used to refer to their struggle. In *Unveiling the Hijab* (2005), Landorf and Pagan wrote about their social studies lesson observation experience of public high school students. The goal was for students to critically examine current issues regarding hijab. They stated that students would compare and contrast the muhajabat experience in France and Iran. The desired results were for "students to come to their own opinion about the meaning of the hijab, the complexity of Islam and different public and private uses of this symbol" (p. 171). This approach to learning about hijab through the public school curriculum, I believe, oversimplifies the issue and minimizes its importance. In addition, the muhajabat experience in Iran and France differ socially, religiously, politically and culturally. In addition, Landorf and Pagan's (2005) approach cannot be considered contributive or transformative (discussed later on in the multicultural section) because their method was not based upon the historical aspect of veiling pertaining to French and Iranian Muslim females. Negating the religious and political differences between these two countries will not result in understanding the facts. Therefore, it is too broad a topic for students to use as a comparative analysis if they are to be left with any real understanding of the muhajabat public school experience that will be beneficial to their growth and development as students and individuals living and being educated in a global society.

In concluding this writing, Landorf and Pagan share that they believe the lesson was successful because the students' natural curiosity was piqued and that it promotes them to think critically. They state that,

"Such an engagement promotes the academic goals of critical analysis, interpretation, problem solving and meaningful learning". (p. 176) Regarding muhajabat and their school experiences, students analyzing or interpreting information does not lend itself to understanding who muhajabat are, why they wear hijab, what their beliefs are, etc. Critical analysis and problem solving are necessary characteristics for any student to possess. Nonetheless, if the school curriculum is going to include lessons about muhajabat and their experiences, I believe it is imperative that it is based upon factual and current information and in the context of the United States hijab experience.

Communities and Hijab

Hijabis being viewed as a minority group within our society is occurring. There are individuals and organizations that are acknowledging their existence and including them in the current struggle to challenge discrimination and welcome tolerance. A female Rabbi in Meckleburg County, North Carolina spearheaded a project in conjunction with the local public school district and a social justice coalition. They produced a video entitled *Souls of Our Students*. The primary goal of this project was to create a video for use by teachers and students, and to sensitize these individuals to the experiences of students who are placed in the following categories: African-American, Latin-American, Asian-American, religious minorities and people with low socioeconomic status. In addition, a facilitator's guide has been compiled and issues of difference in the lives of these students explored.

The school district that collaborated with this project was the very district that three of the participants in my research have attended. This school district consists of approximately 130,000 students, 8,600 teachers and 7,500 additional employees. There is a diverse population of religious congregations, and this project includes religious leaders who reflect the racial, religious and immigrant diversity in the community.

I was honored to be given the opportunity to attend one of the filming sessions for this video. I met Rabbi Judy, who took the time to explain to me how this project came about. She said that at an eight-week course she attended she learned that the city where the school district is located ranked thirty nine out of forty cities in racial stress. The Rabbi said that during this course, a group of African-American clergy discussed racism and its effects with the group. She was apalled by what she heard. All of the students in the course were given a five hundred dollar stipend to work on projects regarding 'white privilege'. The Rabbi was inspired to develop a larger project and pooled resources from grants and clergy to develop a video, curriculum and facilitator's guide to assist in making people aware of diversity and to hopefully accept, encourage and promote understanding of diverse groups, including Muslims. The director of the social justice coalition and the diversity specialist for the school district were also present at this meeting. They both described and displayed their positive sentiments about seeing this project through to fruition.

Souls of Our Students is a wonderful example of how communities can assist schools to improve the social and educational experiences of our students. This project has progressive implications for this school district and communities which may result in increased tolerance, educating individuals outside of the school system and providing an understanding of diversity within communities at large. Rabbi Judy stated, "Beyond the school system, the broader diversity video will be offered to companies and congregations in the district and county to be used as part of their diversity training." This is a project that deserves national attention because it could be a catalyst for promoting diversity, tolerance and reflection in schools all over the nation.

Diversity and tolerance are both characteristics of multiculturalism. Providing students with a multicultural education is a necessity to further understand the muhajabat experience, and to also understand the experiences of other minority groups that are members of our society at large. The following information about multiculturalism defines what it is and details how school curriculum, teaching and classroom components can entwine and work together to provide a comprehensive school experience beneficial to all public and public school students.

Multiculturalism

In addition to curriculum that is specifically written to include muhajabat, a broader worldview that teaches tolerance and acceptance cannot be overlooked. To some educators and persons concerned with equality and social justice, multicultural education is the answer:

> Multicultural education is a continuous, systematic process that will broaden and diversify as it develops. It views a culturally pluralistic society as a positive force that welcomes differences as vehicles for understanding. It includes programs that are systematic in nature; that enhance and preserve cultural distinctions, diversities, and similarities; and that provide individuals with a wide variety of options and alternatives (Association for Supervision and Curriculum Development, 1977, p. 3).

This definition, provided by the ASCD Multicultural Education Commission over twenty years ago, remains a momentous goal for a successful educational course of action.

Multicultural Curriculum

In order to reduce the prejudicial and racist views embedded in our society and schools, a multicultural curriculum is necessary. It is difficult for valuable education to take place in an environment where negative stereotypes and omissions of cultures other than the dominant one are present: "Educators today have a moral responsibility to move beyond the limits of racial context to a social context that embraces humanity without barriers and fears" (Pullen, 2000, p. 44). The moral responsibility that Pullen (2000) refers to remain elusive in some educational environments even today. Students not being taught factual information about a group of people contributes to the breakdown of existing fibers that bind our schools and communities together. Muhajabat, Muslims and people of multi-ethnic backgrounds numbers are steadily increasing in our society. Schools have the ability to address issues related to multiculturalism and diversity positively through learning. We must take advantage of this opportunity.

Schools can begin to eliminate and eradicate false beliefs propagated in our society so that students can learn to respect one another even when major differences exist. They can learn that Middle Eastern Muslim muhajabat, Latino Catholics and European Protestants all have commonalities. Multicultural teaching and curriculum assists us in acknowledging them. For example, a student who is being unkind to the only muhajaba in the classroom may be doing so for several reasons:

1. He or she has not had prior experience with someone from a different race or culture and he/she does not know how to react;
2. He or she may have had a negative experience with a muhajaba;
3. He or she may come from a home that teaches racist or discriminatory behavior;
4. He or she may simply dislike the person as an individual.

Multicultural teaching and education can assist students in dealing with each of the aforementioned scenarios. Educating the student on muhajabat culture, beliefs and experiences can develop empathy, understanding, acceptance and increased knowledge. As Pullen writes, "Racial definitions of who we are and what we think continue to guide, or more appropriately, misguide the way that we treat one another". (2000, p. 44) This is why learning about others and their cultures and lives is important. This facilitates us in building community inside and outside of school.

Traditionally, curriculum has not been inclusive of minorities aside from units in history textbooks that cover topics such as slavery and the civil war. Students of color and individuals outside of the Judeo/Christian culture experience difficulty identifying with some parts of the public school curriculum. Many schools continue to be places where the students are receivers of knowledge deemed important by those in power. The purpose of multiculturalism in schools is to break down stereotypes and encourage self and cultural appreciation within every student. The goals of the multicultural curriculum would dismantle the curriculum that is prejudicial against many students and replace it with one that is inclusive of diversity. Presently, there are teachers and schools across the country working to achieve this goal.

I will address two approaches to multicultural curriculum, the *contributions approach* and the *transformations approach*. During the contributions approach, students learn about achievements of minorities that were excluded from the standard curriculum. The problem with this approach is that ethnic minorities may be viewed as being temporarily or conditionally important: "Although these studies may contribute to multicultural awareness, they may also leave the impression that ethnic issues and events are merely appendages to the nation's development" (Miller, 1999, p. 22). With the transformation approach, the students are able to question various aspects of curriculum from their own perspectives. An example of this is looking at slavery from a slave's perspective. This may contrast with the textbook explanation of this historic tragedy. As Miller states, "This perspective puts an entirely different slant on many historical events of the period and helps students more fully understand the context of these events". (1999, p. 22) Student understanding of how information is sometimes passed on is necessary in order for them to develop skills that will allow them to critique and benefit from the information.

The transformation approach uses source documents (letters, books, etc.) for students to understand historical events. They are then asked to provide explanations about any evident or discovered inconsistencies with the information. This approach includes discussing the source document, and writing first-hand accounts of any common experience between students. The class develops a graph illustrating the frequency of events after hearing all of the accounts. A discussion follows about why students may have had various perspectives about the same event.

Students are given an opportunity to gather additional information about the event. For example: interviewing or collecting written data from witnesses. A culminating activity follows in which class groups are formed and each group writes their own historical account of the event. It is up to the groups to determine how discrepancies will be solved:

> These reports provide the necessary groundwork for a class discussion of the idea that records of historical events are influenced, and often biased, by the backgrounds and perceptual frameworks of both those who observe them (primary sources) and those who later try to interpret the events. By providing practical, hands-on experiences in some of the vital processes of historiography, this project serves as an exciting vehicle to help elementary students become critical connoisseurs of written history (Miller, 1999, p. 23).

Teaching these skills during the elementary years would be beneficial to students' learning development in high school. These approaches to multicultural curriculum may serve as a guide for those who would prefer a definitive method of application. However, there are other views of how multiculturalism can be applied, which may be determined by school and teacher preference.

Multicultural Teaching

According to Marulis (2000), multicultural teaching is "incorporating multiple perspectives and having no absolute truths. It is helping children to see themselves just the way they are". (p. 27) This acceptance of self aids students in developing their self-esteem and fosters positive feelings of acceptance for others. The multicultural curriculum must be tailored to the students on the receiving end. It is sometimes necessary for teachers to recognize that the curriculum cannot be used in the same exact manner for every student. A multicultural classroom can consist of not only curriculum, but also material things representing various cultures, shared expressions in the form of art, toys, and texts. This type of cultural inclusion builds community in the classroom and heightens the opportunity for transfer beyond the classroom. The benefit is that students become prepared to enter a society that includes multiple and diverse backgrounds. Integrating our cultural differences into the classroom and constructing a positive learning environment is essential.

Teachers need support to accomplish this goal. Teacher colleges and universities should be at the forefront of preparing teachers who are qualified to teach in our rapidly changing schools: "Institutions that prepare teachers must be innovative and fearless in implementing creative strategies that are designed to give authentic multicultural experiences to those who need them the most—the teachers who will teach the future, not just future teachers". (Pullen, 2000, p. 46) This means providing multicultural experiences and learning that can be implemented and utilized by teachers.

Teachers need continuous in-service training in learning to teach multiculturally. Pullen (2000) agrees and believes this training should be focused on four specific phases: self—inventory, mini-lectures, multicultural mentoring and mandatory multicultural lessons.

1. *Self-inventory* provides teachers with an assessment of their individual cultural awareness and tolerance. They will receive an assessment designed to assist them with their interpersonal skills.
2. *Mini-lectures* are given by community members of various cultural backgrounds. Students, parents and community leaders also participate.

3. A *multicultural mentoring program* assigns teachers to professionals of a different race or culture who can share experiences and answer questions.
4. *Mandatory multicultural lessons* are pursued only after the first three phases have been completed. The teacher is required to complete a multicultural lesson utilizing their program experiences.

This type of preparation empowers teachers to become comfortable with teaching multiculturally and assists in eliminating the threat that some teachers feel when required to participate in multicultural teaching. These feelings may arise when the teacher has had limited exposure and experience with cultures other than their own. As a precaution, colleges, universities and school districts can provide mandatory training that will positively immerse teachers in the type of teaching necessary to teach students from many different backgrounds. Using teacher in-service days for this purpose would be advantageous.

Oftentimes teaching occurs that is culturally acceptable to the majority: "We know from common sense and research that, as educators, we tend to teach to the world view and promote learning styles that are dominant for us" (Cruz, 1999, p. 17). This kind of teaching limits the opportunity for students who do not fit into the dominant culture. Once we enter into a realm of open cultural understanding, meaningful teaching can occur. When we teach from multiple perspectives, our students benefit from a truly well—rounded teaching-and-learning experience.

The Necessity of Multicultural Classrooms

The notion that multicultural education is necessary only in schools where the population is culturally diverse is false. Some people may believe that exposure to textbooks that include racial and cultural representation or classroom discussions are sufficient to make known to students that people different from themselves are members of society. This concept is unacceptable because it does not foster tolerance, acceptance, acknowledgment or respect within the student, teacher or school community overall. Teachers need to be required to take time to develop their multicultural teaching skills whether or not they are teaching a class consisting of students from multiple cultures: "Ultimately, teachers must become comfortable and aware of the need to be more multicultural in their mindset in order to reconstruct the racial and cultural context that affects our classrooms, board rooms, and family rooms". (Pullen, 2000, p. 46) This will allow us to obtain and use other methods that will enhance cultural understanding on a grand scale. Classrooms should reflect the multicultural awareness teachers possess.

Constituents of a Multicultural Classroom

What constitutes a multicultural classroom is debatable. Teachers must cross the age-old classroom boundaries where children are taught about other countries and carry over to the other side where life experiences, examples, and discussions can occur. This can be accomplished by teachers taking initiative within their classrooms to teach about various cultures and places around the world. Teachers should analyze the methods they employ to provide their students with a rich multicultural education: "Self reflection encourages teachers to determine if they are creating accurate and fair portrayals of diverse groups of people". (Marulis, 2000, p. 27) Some teachers may find self-reflection difficult and may need assistance from co-workers. Schools can provide assistance to teachers to aid them in building the skills necessary to create, develop and teach multicultural lessons. Education experiences for teachers are necessary throughout the school year so that they can become immersed in components related to multiculturalism on a continuum.

Students of all ages benefit from multicultural education. Pullen (2000) suggests that multicultural education begin at an early age: "I propose that we incorporate a multicultural curriculum that is integrated into all content areas, beginning in preschool. This would include an in-depth exploration of racial differences, gender issues, and culture as a whole". (p. 46)

Children at the preschool age are receptive to learning about others and are less judgmental about children being different in comparison to themselves. We can attempt to prepare students to face life in a complex world by teaching multiculturally and not limiting learning by assimilation into dominant cultural norms.

Teachers establishing written classroom goals can assist in facilitating the development and retention of good multicultural curriculum choices. Marulis (2000) gives an example of how important established multicultural goals are. She states,

> My goal is that my classroom will be a welcoming environment open to all students and their ideas. I make conscious choices about books and other teaching materials that enter my classroom. I analyze each resource, and ask myself what it is saying to my students and what values, beliefs, ways of thinking and perspectives it presents. (p. 27)

This is just one example of how significant multicultural goals can be in reference to educating students.

Concerns Regarding Multiculturalism

There are teachers who sing the praises of multicultural education. However, there are others concerned about problems that arise when required to teach in a multicultural environment. Students hail from comparatively different backgrounds that include racial, religious, ethnic, socio-economic and physical differences. There are teachers who believe that focusing upon any of these differences is problematic because it detracts from what the students have in common. Once we have created an environment where multiculturalism is embraced and cultural commonalities, similarities and differences are all connected for the purpose of learning, concerns regarding focusing upon differences can be eliminated. When the curriculum is disconnected and subjects are taught as separate categories, it is difficult to have a classroom where multiculturalism can thrive.

Teachers need support systems when learning to implement multiculturalism in their classrooms. It is necessary for teachers to have access to multicultural networks provided by their schools where issues can be presented, discussed and addressed as regards multicultural education. Classroom teachers need the support of the school administration. Fragmented efforts by school officials, teachers and support staff to utilize multiculturalism in the school community will not yield results beneficial to students or the school at large.

I recognize that schools lacking in diversity or schools with a very small percentage of students outside the dominant school culture are sometimes permeated by a false sense of comfort. They may be ill-prepared to tend to the needs of any minority entering their education community. Utilizing multicultural education methods would allow schools to always be equipped and prepared to educate students from any cultural, ethnic or religious background.

In addition to the above-mentioned critiques, Sleeter (2001) found that there are critics of multiculturalism who view education in the United States as already fair to all public school students. She provides four core complaints voiced by conservatives, which are being advanced as the problem with multicultural education. They are: suspicious origins, the potential for divisiveness, intellectual rigor and solutions to minority student underachievement.

The origins of multicultural education are viewed suspiciously because they are considered by some to be radical and unnecessary. Sleeter (2001) quotes one critic as stating that, "multiculturalism is partly a product of Blacks who 'repudiate the sciences they cannot master' during a time when scientific culture is dominant". (p. 83) This attitude attempts to minimize and eradicate any undertakings to institute new educational policies representative of the education population as a whole. Multicultural education is being considered divisive because of an emphasis on race and ethinicity. Some critics believe that the curriculum does not have to be race-conscious. Sleeter (2001) expounds on this view by sharing that these critics believe the common culture of public education in the United States is inclusive and universal. They believe that "the purpose of schooling is to cultivate reason so that citizens can rise above their own particular circumstances and participate rationally in a common culture". (p. 84)

What these critics fail to realize is that the "common culture" has not sufficiently included the contributions of minorities socially or academically, which is one relevant reason why multiculturalism is a necessity.

The argument about multicultural curriculum being intellectually weak is unsubstantiated and is by and large supported by those whose sentiments cite diversity curricula and courses as lacking scholarship. New York City's multicultural curriculum has come under attack for being weak scholarship. "Its interest in history is not as an intellectual discipline but rather as social and psychological therapy whose primary function is to raise the self-esteem of children from minority group". (Sleeter, 2001, p. 84) These critics view multiculturalism as being promoted by African Americans to assuage their feelings of inadequacy and their alleged desire to be paid back for their slavery ancestry. This mindset precedes the fourth complaint against multiculturalism that cites student underachievement.

Critics of multicultural education believe that multiculturalism seeks to replace real academic achievement with "self-esteem exercises" for minority student underachievers. They believe that low-expectations become institutionalized and are inherent in multicultural education. These racist, uninformed and ignorant beliefs provide an example of how racial or religious minorities can be confounded by the educational institutions they attend. Examining the muhajabat school experience in the context of the multicultural debate provides an important look at how racism, inequality and public education form a complex relationship in need of critical analysis and debate to serve as a catalyst for positive educational change that will be inclusive of people from all racial, religious and ethnic origins.

In order for students to truly have a multicultural education, their curriculum and social environments must include multiple cultures, experiences and opportunities. It had been thought that including Martin Luther King Day, Black History Month and Native American units or themes created a culturally diverse experience for students. We now know that achieving multiculturalism requires more. Otherwise, schools fall short in preparing students with knowledge, skills and understandings necessary for success in this diverse world.

As a component to educating students multiculturally, America's public schools should also be responsible for educating students about religions and people of the world, and this includes Islam. School libraries should be inclusive of books containing accurate information about Muslims and Islam as well as fiction books written by Muslim authors. I have compiled a list (see appendix H) of books commonly used in libraries that are representational of Muslims and Islam. Educating students about Islam and Muslims is essential because it helps to demonstrate that they are members of our schools, communities and American culture and society at large.

In a North Carolina public library, I asked a librarian for assistance in locating a book. We began conversing and discussing my research.

She smiled and said, "I have an article for you." She explained that she had listened to an author, who was also a Muslim' speak, and that she kept one of the author's articles in her desk. The author is Khan (2006) and the article is entitiled, *Muslims in Children's Books*. Khan explains the importance of having literary works that are truly representational of Muslims and what Muslim culture has to offer. Khan states, "In the best of times, it is extremely difficult to write about another culture in a truthful and sensitive manner". (2006, pp. 36-37) However, in today's political climate it is increasingly important. She suggests books for children that can be placed in five categories: contemporary picture books, contemporary novels, short stories, folktales and nonfiction. Khan's text suggestions are useful to schools and libraries because it provides a starting point for the ones whose multicultural text are not inclusive of Islam and Muslim people.

I would like to conclude this chapter with the influential words of Loren Marulis (2000) who expressively imparts the following:

> Multiculturalism must be immersed into a classroom and curriculum. It must be all encompassing. It is not only taught through formal lessons, but is modeled and demonstrated at all times. In a classroom where multicultural teaching is embraced and implemented, all students feel represented, respected, celebrated, and safe. They feel like their voice is heard and appreciated. Multicultural teaching is creating an environment that says, 'everyone is welcome here'. (p. 27)

the above-mentioned educational and learning environment can have a powerful impact on the public school experiences of muhajabat and students in general.

CHAPTER VII

CONCLUSION

The conclusion of this book is a significant constituent of this research because of the strengths and weaknesses that became evident. These findings allows for decisions to be made regarding muhajabat and their experiences in relation to the public and public school endurances.

Research Implications

Goffman's (1963) theories regarding social identity were fundamentally important to this research. Most, if not all, of the literature regarding muhajabat in the West utilizes feminist theory as the vehicle for needed change for these females. This can be a source of contention or debate between Muslims, educators, politicians and social activists. Whether or not an individual agrees with feminist ideologies becomes insignificant when social identity is the grounding device used to truly understand and comprehend some of the muhajabat school experiences.

The tribal stigmas these muhajabat bear have made some of them susceptible to unwanted feelings of alienation and estrangement from their school community. Feelings of alienation arise when muhajabat become aware of being outcasts in their social environments. This research demonstrates how negative experiences in schools trigger the devaluing of oneself; altering of beliefs, customs, and practices in public settings; social withdrawal; family, religious and/or cultural rejection;

and a negative impact on identity. It also provides tangible examples of how strength, pride and self-valuing contribute to student success irrespective of negative school experiences that have occurred. This is why I believe that using identity and social interaction theories to become informed about the experiences and emotions muhajabat face as stigmatized individuals is central. Coupled with muhajabat theory, understanding what these females believe and why they do so can assist with providing solutions to the problems they face as public school students. Incorporating various facets of muhajabat's lives, beliefs, and prior experiences is a requisite for continuous development of this theory so that Muslims and researchers are able to acknowledge it as sufficient to explain and provide an understanding of the muhajabat experience. There are many theories that can be applied to human phenomena but they do not encompass an understanding of the Muslim belief system on which diverse facets of many Muslim lives are determined. The purpose of hijab theory is to provide this important link. Hijab theory, along with Goffman's (1961, 1963, 1967) theories, are components of this research's strengths.

In addition, there were three questions developed in the methodology section that are central to this study and of great importance. They are:

1. How do you feel about being a muhajaba in public school?
2. What are some of the experiences you have had that you would deem positive or negative?
3. How can teachers and principals assist muhajabat in having an improved educational experience?

The presentation of these questions brings to light additional information that is crucial. Although the questions are general, they elicited feedback that was necessary to enter into the realm of analysis by the researcher and the muhajabat themselves.

Muhajabat attending public schools are a unique group. As an adolescent muhajaba it is difficult to objectively consider the ramifications or possible difficulties one will have to face and the resulting effects due to immaturity, lack of social exposure and a host of other growth and development factors. This is why I chose to also use surveys completed by professional Muslims, muhajabat women and mothers. The concerns of most of the women regarding muhajabat attending public schools were validated by the muhajabat interviews. These professional women and mothers were able to consider the salient possibilities that being in a public school environment could conjure for these females. When considered outside the context of this research, the survey responses can seem like unwarranted fears that display a desire to limit socialization with non-Muslims. Juxtaposing the issues presented by the women who completed the surveys with the muhajabat interviewed brings forth a wealth of understanding that all of these components are interconnected, relevant and of great import.

Research Limitations

Having a process and specific methods mapped out to conduct this research was not sufficient. While completing interviews and observations, it became apparent that there were recognizable limitations due to the age of the muhajabat (15 years in contrast to 19 years) and social experience (exposed to non-Muslims or Muslims comparatively different from themselves in various public settings). These are both important correlates as to how muhajabat recognize, understand and inevitably comprehend their experiences. Focusing on their social transitions as students in junior high school, high school, college & university is not only relevant, it is necessary. Muhajabat school experiences evolve as they mature and transition in their role as veiled students in American society. How they perceive people and how they are perceived will impact their lives.

Examples of the above information emerged during the interview and research process. During my initial interview with Amina, she mentions that her teachers "really don't talk to me." When I asked her why she thought that was, she shrugs and deduces that maybe it was because she did not speak to them. When I ask her why her teachers thought that was, she looks surprised and informs me that she did not speak to them about it. Whether it was due to her age or comfort level or both, Amina did not pursue or present this question to her teachers. Being a muhajaba or being a muhajaba student never came up in this particular conversation. I cannot help but wonder what would have happened if she had posed the question to her teachers about having limited or no conversation with them in comparison to the other students. What sort of information would have emerged? This type of student initiated follow—up with a teacher has occurred in research regarding Muslim students as mentioned in the article *Aisha and Her Multiple Identities*. (Chaudhry, 2005) Aisha was a student at a University of California campus who participated in an ethnographic study about life's complexities for a Pakistani Muslim woman in the United States. Having difficulty with an art teacher whom she felt did not acknowledge her completed assignments, Aisha decided to speak to him about his treatment of her. Chaudhry accompanied her to his office and waited outside. When Aisha emerged from the professor's office, she sadly informed her that, "My veil intimidates him, and he can't relate to me". (Chaudhry, 2005, p. 540) Aisha's pursuit of this line of questioning brought forth a tumult of thoughts surrounding being a muhajaba. These thoughts probably would not have occurred had it not been for her experience and follow-up. This is something some adolescent muhajabat may not think to do or may consciously avoid.

As muhajabat students grow and become comfortable in their educational and social environments, the ways in which they address challenging experiences will diversify. I will go so far as to say that muhajabat can be divided into three categories: girl, adolescent and woman with sub-categories under woman based upon their life experiences and worldly exposure. In other words, these categories can be contextualized based upon age and socialization. The experiences of muhajabat in these various categories differ. For example, the American Muslim female experience as worshippers, citizens, minorities and an array of other classifications is provided thoughtfully by Ulen (2005) in *Shattering the Stereotypes, Muslim Women Speak Out*. What makes this book chapter germane to this research is Ulen's descriptive analysis and admiration for muhajabat. Although she does not cite Muslim injunctions regarding hijab, she deems it an important issue regardless of the fact that she only wears hijab when praying. Ulen compels the reader to look through an alternate social lens to understand another perspective or gain further insight about the importance to Muslim women. Ulen writes:

> I want more non-Muslims to understand veiled Muslim women and respect them for celebrating Muslim creed, for resisting overwhelming economic forces in this country, for not succumbing to the images captured in high fashion gloss.

By living in constant alignment with faith, they challenge the
misogynist systems that compel too many Western women
and girls to binge, purge, and starve themselves. For these
pious sisters, plain cloth is the most meaningful accessory
they could ever wear . . . In the context of consumerist
America, women who cover express power of intellect over
silhouette, of mind over matters of the flesh. (p. 46)

Astounding! I have been wearing hijab for most of my life, I have
attended two colleges and a university and I am a doctoral graduate.
Why then have I been so ignorant to the many facets of hijab? My
only answer to this question is social experience. Ulen is a Muslim
convert who was awarded a 2004 Presidential Award for Teaching.
She is a faculty member at Hunter College. She has received fiction-
writing fellowships from the Frederick Douglass Creative Arts Center
and the Provincetown Fine Arts Work Center, and the list goes on.
Her assertions regarding hijab describe a very social-political thought
process. Although I appreciate her writing, the depth and diversity of
her thoughts regarding Muslim women wearing hijab are not necessarily
interchangeable with Muslim female girls or adolescents. As a matter of
fact, it would be difficult for me to even imagine Aisha (UC student)
or Reem (one of the muhajaba interviewed) sharing this perspective. As
muhajabat youth ponder and contemplate their experiences as female
Muslims who wear hijab, American fashion images in contradiction to
the Muslim faith are most likely an issue that will arise and have already
arisen for some of the research participants. However, some of the
muhajabat who are focused upon in this study have yet to make some
of the complex connections regarding hijab and their social experiences.
Therefore, age and social experience must be taken into consideration
when discussing muhajabat and their public school experiences.

Alleviating some of the concerns mentioned above could possibly
be addressed through moral and ethical education as Noddings (1984)
suggests. If caring and ethical education were inclusive within the K-12
curriculum, it may have a positive impact upon how muhajabat or any
students are treated by one another. However, without this type of
curriculum integration, I have deduced that it would probably not make
a large contribution to positive experiences for muhajabat in public
schools. After analyzing the experiences of Amina, Kamillah, Sumaiya,

Saadia, Asma and Reem, I would have to say that the entire educational system would have to be in agreement and willing to accept the caring model theory. Henceforth, spirituality may provide an opportunity for individuals to improve their personal well-being while promoting human acceptance, but it is not a solution that will benefit the general school population because it would require understanding and personal commitment.

As mentioned earlier in the research, my original decision to use photographs was made because muhajabat students are a relatively new topic being discussed in relation to public schools. When speaking to educators or those in related fields, I was continuously posed with the question, "What is a muhajabat?" I believed that photographs would help answer this question. This was not the case. Perhaps this experience is what Walker (1999) was referring to when he states, "When we do encounter photographs, we are at a loss with what to do with them". (p. 39) When some individuals viewed the photographs, the perceived races of the muhajabat replaced the hijab as the focus. I then began to ponder the question, "Is skin color relevant and if so, why"? The hijab is part of a Muslim way of life, not a racial way of life. Perhaps the relevant question becomes, does race play a determining role in how a muhajabat is perceived and treated? This question is another topic in itself. Nonetheless, the photographs seemed to hinder the connection to the muhajabat experience that I attempted to make. It became more of a limitation than a positive contribution.

Regarding the interviews, neither Amina, Kamillah, Sumaiya, Saadia, Asma nor Reem referred to their race as a possible indicator or reason for uncomfortable public school experiences. Being a Muslim who wears hijab was the crux of their educational and social circumstances lived. Therefore, I did not focus upon pursuing the issue of race in the context of these females being muhajabat and attending public schools. For some people today, the vast mixture of their racial heritage is a contributing factor to a growing belief that race has become a subjective category of irrelevant information and even an unfair categorization that can leave harmful effects. If the muhajabat themselves addressed the issue of race and racism, I would have delved further into their feelings and emotions regarding this belief. This did not occur. Therefore, I centralized the research around their identity and social experiences.

Goffman's (1961, 1963, 1967) theories pertaining to stigma and interaction assist in providing understanding with regard to the muhajabat experience. However, Goffman's stigma and spoiled identity theories were limited and insufficient to explain how an individual who has suffered from tribal stigma or unpopular affiliations could emerge from negative experiences emotionally and psychologically unscathed. Saadia and Reem were prime examples of individuals not being consumed by their stigma of muhajabat status. Although they endured several negative educational and social experiences, they were able to overcome them without internalizing them or allowing the negativity to permeate their lives. Goffman's sociological theories did not take into account the possibility of individuals who live with a stigma being able to resist the effects of stigmatization.

An additional limitation was the small number of participants. Although the research participants ages and cultural backgrounds were diverse, having only six committed participants may have reduced the content and span of information that I would have been able to receive regarding the muhajabat experience if I were able to acquire a larger number of participants. However, having only a limited number of participants by no means negates the important and relevant information and data that was collected and analyzed for this study.

Final Thoughts

If people continue to approach muhajabat as females who choose to look different rather than females practicing their faith, then the communication gap between Muslims and non—Muslims with regard to this subject will continue to widen, and the chains of prejudice and discrimination will be strengthened. Fewer Muslims will place themselves in a position to discuss hijab, because the political and social climate of our country has already made a negative determination about its value. Identity will forever play a role in the lives of muhajabat, particularly those living in non-Muslim societies, or even Muslim societies endeavoring to become westernized.

The topic of Muslim females who wear hijab will most likely continue to evolve, expand and flourish as a subject with many points for debate and discussion. It is unlikely that this topic will disappear in the near future. I would like to expand my research regarding muhajabat by learning more about American Muslim females who wear hijab in the workplace, particularly professional women including, but not limited to, doctors, lawyers, teachers, nurses and social workers. I am committed to pursuing this next phase of muhajabat.

Appendices

The following surveys were developed to gather multiple opinions regarding Muslim female muhajabat attending public schools. These surveys demonstrate the concern that some Muslim females and mothers have with regard to Muslim children attending public school. The majority of the females surveyed believe that Muslim children should not attend public school because their identity and religious beliefs will be compromised. Concerns regarding male and female intermingling in public schools, and the lack of education pertaining to Muslim culture not only emerged from the surveys, but also the interviews with muhajabat attending public schools. These concerns are both relevant and legitimate and can be understood after reviewing the interview excerpts and the information shared by the muhajabat.

Appendix A

SURVEY I—MUSLIM PRINCIPALS

1. 33 year old Egyptian

   How long have you been Muslim? I was born Muslim

   Do you have children? Two

   If so, do they attend a public or private Muslim school? Muslim school

   Why? To teach her the Muslim rules

   Do you believe Muslim children should attend public schools? Why or why not?

   She must understand her identity first. She can get exposed to the American style but this is of course after putting them in Muslim elementary schools. I want them to be independent, able to think for themselves.

   Are there any questions, concerns, or personal information that you could share pertaining to Muslim females who observe hijab and attend public schools? No

2. 42 years old African American

    How long have you been Muslim? Eleven years

    Do you have children? No

    Do you believe Muslim children should attend public schools? Why or why not?

    I do not feel that Muslim children should attend public school because I feel that children are not given individualized attention. Children attending Muslim schools benefit because they receive both Muslim and public together.

    Are there any questions, concerns, or personal information that you could share pertaining to Muslim females who observe hijab and attend public schools?

    Girls attending public schools, who wear hijab find it extremely difficult due to the teasing that they experience. Often girls are fearful of attending school because of the teasing.

3. 32 years old Guyanese

    How long have you been Muslim? I was born Muslim

    Do you have children? Three

    If so, do they attend a public or private Muslim school? Muslim school

    Why? Need for Muslim values and principles

    Do you believe Muslim children should attend public schools? Why or why not?

    No. No discipline there

Are there any questions, concerns, or personal information that you could share pertaining to Muslim females who observe hijab and attend public schools?

Be proud of who you are no matter where you may be (Muslim/non Muslim school, Muslim/non Muslim environment). Know in your heart of hearts the hijab is a public statement of who you are. I didn't wear hijab in public school, and I still felt alienated and out of place as a Muslim. I skipped school because I didn't want to be in the environment.

4. 50 years old Egyptian

    How long have you been Muslim? Born Muslim

    Do you have children? Two sons

    If so, do they attend a public school or private Muslim school?

    A private Muslim school

    Why? Because of the Muslim environment

    Do you believe Muslim children should attend public schools? Why or why not?

    No. They need a Muslim environment

    Are there any questions, concerns, or personal information that you could share pertaining to Muslim females who observe hijab and attend public schools?

    Muslim girls should keep their Islam seen.

Even with a sample of only four participants, answers varied from one end of the spectrum (Muslims should not attend public school) to another (after Muslim children learn about being Muslim) they can attend public school. The responses to these questions demonstrate the diversity of Muslim thought and female experiences and opinions with regard to education. I specifically asked female, Muslim muhajabat principals these questions to see if this specific category of muhajabat regarded public and private Muslim education in the same way with regard to Muslim children and muhajabat.

Appendix B

SURVEY II—CONFERENCE PARTICIPANTS

1. **Age:** 35 years

   State: Tennessee

   What is your nationality? African American, Puerto Rican and Dominican

   How long have you been Muslim? Three years

   How long have you been wearing hijab? Off and on for sixteen years/steady for three years

   Did you attend public or private school? Public school

   Did you wear hijab while in attendance at school? No, however, my daughter did before she started home schooling

   What were your experiences like? My daughter was often ridiculed and was even pushed down in the hallway by a young man and told to go back to Pakistan. On the flipside, a lot of her female companions became very interested in Islam. Most of my experiences are conversations about why we cover which I like to take the opportunity to give *dawwah* (educating people about Islam) and dispel the myths and ignorance.

How did you feel about being a muhajabat in school (elementary, high school, college)?

My daughter felt very proud and so do I. I feel like royalty and my daughter has told me that she is a Muslim Diva Princess. When we first became Muslim three years ago, I did not force my daughter to cover, although I did immediately. I allowed her the opportunity to decide to cover on her own. Eight months later, she came to me and declared that she was ready to start completely covering because she understood the importance of being modest.

Do you believe Muslim children should attend public schools? Why or why not?

I do not believe Muslim children should attend public schools because my spiritual guide has directed our community against it. Even before knowledge of this, I was opposed to this because our children are corrupted by false teachings, oppositional behavior and ideologies, food restricted to Muslims, lack of support (i.e. not being permitted time to make prayer or be excused from school for Muslim holidays).

Are there specific issues that muhajabat face when they are in a non-Muslim environment? Absolutely. We are sometimes looked at oddly, however, I have found that there are generally one of two responses; either people are extremely drawn and attracted to us or they are repelled and hateful. Many people are curious and hijab becomes a opening for conversation which I take advantage of for dawwah. I am way more vigilant about being protected spiritually in non—Muslim environments and also about representing Islam properly.

What can educators do to provide muhajabat with a positive school experience?

Become culturally aware about Muslim practices. The Muslim communities have to approach school boards and tactfully demand that they become sensitive to the needs of Muslim children attending school. The boards will listen because Muslim are now viable, tax paying, community members. We can then hold classes at the schools with staff and faculty to address the needs of our children i.e. more diverse menus, time to allow for prayer, giving an understanding of hijab so girls are not penalized for not dressing a certain way for physical education and allowing excused absences for our holidays.

2. **Age:** 26

State: South Carolina

What is your nationality? Black

How long have you been Muslim? Born

How long have you been wearing hijab? Sixteen years. **Did you attend public or private school?** Yes, public. **Did you wear hijab in attendance at school?** Yes.

What were your experiences like? It was very good because people were asking where they could get Muslim clothing and if I could sew them some thing. I liked the feeling from having this happen.

How did you feel about being a muhajabat in school (elementary, high school, college)?

It was very nice because you get a lot of respect when you are dressed Islamically.

Do you believe Muslim children should attend public schools? Why or why not? No, they should not because they may lose their religion. There are so many things in the schools that are not good which affect our children.

Are there specific issues that muhajabat face when they are in a non-Muslim environment?

Some people discriminate against Muslims.

What can educators do to provide muhajabat with a positive school experience? They can stop portraying us as oppressed and abused women.

3. **Age:** 23

   State: New York City

   What is your nationality? Eastern European

   How long have you been Muslim? All my life (23 years).

   How long have you been wearing hijab? All my life.

   Did you attend public or private school? Public.

   Did you wear hijab while in attendance at school? Yes.

   What were your experiences like? My experiences were fine. As a matter of fact, although I was aware of the fact that I was Muslim in a predominately non-Muslim environment, I felt as though I was relatively accepted.

   How did you feel about being a muhajabat in school (elementary, high school, college)?

   I felt fine, especially when I was having a typical teenage day.

   Do you believe Muslim children should attend public schools? Why or why not?

   Now that I am a little older and have a more, broader perspective of Islam, I sometimes wish that I hadn't been exposed to certain things that I wouldn't have normally been privy to as a attendee at a Muslim run school.

Are there specific issues that muhajabat face when they are in a non-Muslim environment? Prying, curious stares and I had a couple of pranksters who tried to take my scarf off. The principal, once he was made aware of it, was so disturbed that he dealt with the individuals in a just way and not other problems arose.

What can educators do to provide muhajabat with a positive school experience? Make sure that all aspects of religious culture are taught to students. This should be done in a way where it is understood that the lessons aren't for converting purposes, but for increasing peoples understanding especially since there is so much going on in regard to Muslims today.

4. **Age:** 24

State: California

What is your nationality? African American and White.

How long have you been Muslim? Ten years.

How long have you been wearing hijab? Ten years.

Did you attend public or private school? Public.

Did you wear hijab while in attendance at school? Yes.

What were your experiences like? I had a very good experience pertaining to wearing hijab in school. I had a more welcoming attitude from the people. My popularity actually increased.

How did you feel about being a muhajabat in school (elementary, high school, college)? It was only uncomfortable for a small period of time. It actually helped my self-confidence.

Do you believe Muslim children should attend public schools? Why or why not?

No. I do not believe that Muslim children should attend public school because it is not good for their religious beliefs. The music, dancing, promiscuity and intermingling is against the Muslim social code.

Are there specific issues that muhajabat face when they are in a non-Muslim environment?

Automatic standoffishness, intimidation, rude comments and ignorance.

What can educators do to provide muhajabat with a positive school experience? Do not treat them differently and respect their beliefs.

5. **Age:** 34

    State: Virginia

    What is your nationality? African American

    How long have you been Muslim? Sixteen years.

    How long have you been wearing hijab? Sixteen years.

    Did you attend public or private school? Public

    Did you wear hijab while in attendance at school? Yes.

    What were your experiences like? I had an enlightening experience while wearing hijab in school. In the beginning people, out of ignorance, made jokes but later students realized that I was offended and eventually asked questions. I explained how it was my belief and they understood and really appreciated that I expressed my beliefs.

    How did you feel about being a muhajabat in school (elementary, high school, *college*)? Wearing hijab in college is the same as wearing hijab to the store or to the doctor or visiting a relative. My hijab is a part of me.

Do you believe Muslim children should attend public schools? Why or why not?

I don't believe Muslim children should attend public schools if other academic schooling is available. Muslim children need time to grow within their belief system instead of being confused with opposing values that public school teach.

Are there specific issues that muhajabat face when they are in a non-Muslim environment?

Muhajabat may face issues of prejudice remarks, unfair treatment and ridicule.

What can educators do to provide muhajaba with a positive school experience?

Educators can bridge the gap between muhajabat and non-muhajabat by making sure students are treated equally therefore, making muhajabat school experiences a positive one.

6. **Age:** 35

   State: Tennessee

   What is your nationality? African American

   How long have you been Muslim? Eighteen years.

   Did you attend public or private school? Public

   Did you wear hijab while in attendance at school? Yes.

   What were your experiences like? Pleasant

How did you feel about being a muhajabat in school (elementary, high school, college)?

I feel fine. Since the war in Iraq I have gotten more questions from other students about Islam.

Do you believe Muslim children should attend public schools? Why or why not?

No, if the school does not allow the child to practice some of the basics of Islam such as making their prayers on time, meeting dietary needs, etc.

Are there specific issues that muhajabat face when they are in a non-Muslim environment?

(Participant left this question blank).

What can educators do to provide muhajabat with a positive school experience?

Educators can first, with any pupil, get to know the students they educate!

7. **Age:** 34

   State: Mississippi

   What is your nationality? African American

   How long have you been Muslim? Eighteen years.

   How long have you been wearing hijab? Eighteen years. **Did you attend public or private school?** Public school **Did you wear hijab while in attendance at school?** Yes.

   What were your experiences like? It was interesting. I am so happy I had my sisters there with me. By wearing a hijab, I got a lot of interesting questions. For example, are you bald headed? What would you do if I pulled that off of you?

How did you feel about being a muhajabat is school (elementary, high school, college)?

I felt ok. In my case I became Muslim in the middle of the school year so the kids were like "I saw your hair before. Why are you covering it now"? Also, I got to 'really' know these people who called themselves friends. The ones I thought would still hang around left. Those that I thought would leave remained my friends.

Do you believe Muslim children should attend public schools? Why or why not?

No, because the peer pressure is so strong.

Are there specific issues that muhajabat face when they are in a non-Muslim environment? Yes. Because of people's lack of knowledge, they ask questions that make one uncomfortable. **What can educators do to provide muhajabat with a positive school experience?**

Have the student explain why they wear the hijab.

8. **Age:** 25

   State: Michigan

   What is your nationality? African American **How long have you been Muslim?** All of my life **Did you attend public or private school?** Public

   Did you wear hijab while in attendance at school? Yes.

   What were your experiences like? I got many questions about, "That thing on my head". But usually these questions were often positive. Many times I had long discussions with my fellow students about the honor of a lady.

How did you feel about being a muhajabat in school (*elementary, high school, college*)?

I didn't think about it. This is a normal part of my dress. That's like saying "How do you feel when you put on your shoe"? However, if no one else wears shoes, they may stare. But my hijab is so much a part of me that I wonder why they are staring at first.

Do you believe Muslim children should attend public schools? Why or why not?

No, because public schools do not teach Muslim culture.

Are there specific issues that muhajabat face when they are in a non-Muslim environment?

The main issue is being able to answer questions in an educated, positive way.

What can educators do to provide muhajabat with a positive school experience? Education is what is needed to make the experiences more positive. Knowing the honor the hijab carries cuts down many problems.

9. **Age:** 29

   State: North Carolina

   What is your nationality? American

   How long have you been Muslim? Twelve years.

   How long have you been wearing hijab? Twelve years.

   Did you attend public or private school? Public

Did you wear hijab while in attendance at school? Yes.

What were your experiences like? My scarf was snatched off my head at times. It was hard but as I grew older I was treated like the other students.

How did you feel about being a muhajabat in school (elementary, high school, college)?

At first it was hard but once the public became familiar with me, and Islam it was easier.

Do you believe Muslim children should attend public schools? Why or why not?

No because of the negative influence public schools have on their lives.

Are there specific issues that muhajabat face when they are in a non-Muslim environment?

Yes, we constantly have to explain ourselves to others and prove that we are good people.

What can educators do to provide muhajabat with a positive school experience?

Show pictures and advertisements with muhajaba to make others more aware of Muslims and their dress.

10. **Age:** 29

State: Michigan

What is your nationality? Afro American.

How long have you been Muslim? Born Muslim

Did you attend public or private school? Public

Did you wear hijab while in attendance at school? Yes.

What were your experiences like? I was always an outsider.

How did you feel about being a muhajaba in school (elementary, high school, college)?

In elementary school, I felt shy, small and as an outsider. In college and vocational tech. it was fine. People wanted to be like me.

Do you believe Muslim children should attend public schools? Why or why not?

No, not in elementary or high school because when you are the minority it is too stressful for a child to deal with.

Are there specific issues that muhajabat face when they are in a non-Muslim environment? Ridicule to a certain degree from other students and teachers, and constant reminders that you are different, self-esteem being beaten down.

What can educators do to provide muhajabat with a positive school experience?

Paying special attention to these students and making other students aware of why Muslim ladies wear hijab.

11. **Age:** 54

    State: Tennessee

    What is your nationality? American

    How long have you been Muslim? Nearly thirty years.

    How long have you been wearing hijab? Nearly thirty years.

    Did you attend public or private school? Neither.

Did you wear hijab while in attendance at school? N/A

What were your experiences like? I attended college as a muhajabat but only for a few weeks. I don't recall much of a problem. This was thirty some years ago.

How did you feel about being a muhajabat in school (elementary, high school, college)?

I have no problem asserting myself as a Muslim in any way at any time or place. Be prepared for the issues mentioned in the second question that follows below.

Do you believe Muslim children should attend public schools? Why or why not? No. The non-Muslim influence and the agenda behind their education, some of their text, teachers, are damaging to the beliefs and culture of Muslims

Are there specific issues that muhajabat face when they are in a non-Muslim environment?

Yes, discrimination, ridicule and rejection.

What can educators do to provide muhajabat with a positive school experience? Educate non-muhajabat as to the letter and spirit of hijab. Support muhajabat in their dress.

12. **Age:** 33

State: South Carolina

What is your nationality? Asian/Indian

How long have you been Muslim? Thirty-three years.

How long have you been wearing hijab? Twenty-nine years.

Did you attend public or private school? Both

Did you wear hijab while in attendance at school? Yes.

What were your experiences like? Good for the most part. My fifth grade teacher informed the class on day one that this was a part of her religion do not disrespect her or snatch her veil or you will be punished.

How did you feel about being a muhajabat in school (*elementary*, high school, *college*)?

I felt ok, yet slight anxiety initially. But it disappeared after the first two weeks or so. **Do you believe Muslim children should attend public schools? Why or why not?** No I do not. It will compromise their religion.

Are there specific issues that muhajabat face when they are in a non-Muslim environment? That we are terrorists, and we are extremely hot with all of our clothes. No to both statements **What can educators do to provide muhajabat with a positive school experience?**

Educate the students about why we dress this way. Knowledge is everything and ignorance is where you have problems.

Appendix C

IDENTITY RESPONSES

After providing information about my research, I posted the following question on a Muslim educator's website: 'How would you define Muslim identity'? During the research phase of social and psychological theories and interview outcomes, issues of identity emerged. I was unable to formulate a specific list of characteristics that are specific to Muslim identity so I decided to ask other Muslims how they would define this. I received the following five responses from one male and four females.

1. Female

I am German and became Muslim almost twenty years ago. I am now forty-two years old. I think Muslim identity is before all things identifying your self as a Muslim, i.e. a follower of the religion of Islam, i.e. following the teachings of the Qur'an as a divine revelation and the Sunna as the teachings of the Prophet(s) who Muslims consider their example in life. Being Muslim for me is more important than nationality because someone can be Muslim regardless of his/her nationality, race, social status, etc.

In a wider sense, Muslim identity is also linked to your culture—if you are a born Muslim. As a Muslim convert you get exposed to several cultures as you interact with Muslims, but you don't necessarily identify yourself with them as they can sometimes go against Muslim teachings.

2. Male

As Salam alaykum,

That simple statement above, "God's peace upon you", written or spoken in Arabic by one Muslim to another is an invitation, or offer, to contract both parties will interact with each other Islamically. "Wa Alaykum assalaam" is the acceptance of the offer, which means we now have established a contract to deal with each other in accordance with Islam. Muslim identity is now established.

To me, that is Muslim identity in a nutshell. Others may not believe what we say, but they trust what we do. We do so calmly and with humility, praying that the Almighty is pleased with our behavior and that we fare well Insh'Allah (If it is the will of God) on the Judgement Day.

3. Female

Muslim identity to me is when Islam takes precedence before any other groups that you may claim allegiance to (i.e. nationality). When one lives life, regardless of man-made boundaries, as a Muslim at all times then they are beginning the Muslim identity formation. That identity is not something that you work at, it just becomes your identity when your salat becomes a part of you, when the Sunnah and Qur'an are your turn-to books, when your role models become the Prophet PBUH, sahabah and other Muslims who you feel emulate a good Muslim. Muslim identity becomes a badge of honor that one feels proud to wear, not shy or ashamed of, or defensive of.

4. Female.

In reference to your question on Muslim identity: I think that Muslim children who go to public schools must have a very strong support system from not only their parents but extended family or friends to form a strong Muslim identity. I have seen opposite ends of both spectrums.

To me, defining Muslim identity is defining who we are. Being Muslim is part of our identity. Therefore, we can't escape it because as Muslims we should take the whole package . . . not bits and pieces from the religion that we choose to follow.

I empathize with the young Muslim children who go to public schools. They are forced to take part in traditions and customs that are not part of their culture but often times adverse to it. When I say forced . . . I mean that although they do not participate . . . the belief system is constantly enveloping them. For example, my children do not partake in the music program. Although in the past, teachers have been gracious enough to allow my children to join another class or use the computer during music, this year my daughter is forced to sit in the office and wait until music is over. During the Christmas holiday concert she became very upset when she realized she would not be performing with her classmates.

I work in a Muslim School and I see the difference with my students. They are only in 1st grade but have a very strong identity, sense of self, and love and crave Muslim teachings and lessons. It is a pleasure to see such strong faith in these young children. I think your next question could be, 'How does public school effect Muslim identity'?

5. Female

I am a thirty-eight, white female, and I converted to Islam fifteen years ago Alhamdulillah (All praise is due to God).

When we talk about developing a "Muslim identity" in our children (and our selves), we are trying to establish Islam as our own world-view, through which our actions are guided, our opinions are formed, and our values are shaped. Islam becomes our measure for fundamental questions for what is "right" and "wrong", and we come to realize the true purpose of our existence, which is only to serve Allah.

ARTICLES

The following articles were mentioned in chapter one. They provide a comprehensive example of how the hijab debate has developed into an American social-political issue that can no longer be viewed as 'foreign' to our country. Examining our perspectives as Americans regarding this topic has become necessary. Law makers, politicians, educators and the average citizen are beginning to face the reality that the hijab controversy will not quietly disappear.

1. February 20, 2004   Associated Press
   Riley Administration Change Rules on Head Scarves

2. June 17, 2005   Herald News
   Muslim Student's Rights Violated

3. March 6, 2006   Des Moines Register
   Muslim Woman Denied Job for Scarf Sues

4. October 2, 2001   Charlotte Observer
   Muslim Girls Find Solidarity, Togetherness in Troop 1101

Appendix D

RILEY ADMINISTRATION CHANGES RULES ON HEAD SCARVES

MONTGOMERY, Ala. (AP)—Responding to complaints from Muslim women, Gov. Bob Riley's administration is changing a policy that prohibited the wearing of head scarves in driver's license photos.

The new policy says head coverings and headgear are acceptable for religious beliefs and medical conditions, but for no other reason.

State Public Safety Director Mike Coppage said his department was delivering the rule change to county probate judges on Friday, and that it would take effect Monday.

Muslim women who had complained were glad to see the state's quick response. "This is a victory for religious freedom for everyone in this country," said LaTonya Floyd of Mobile.

The new policy requires that the face be visible from the top of the forehead to the bottom of the chin and from the hairline on one side to the hairline on the other side.

Troy King, the governor's legal adviser, said the change would maintain the state's goal of being able to identify a person from a driver's license photo while being respectful of people's religious beliefs and traditions.

The state Department of Public Safety issued new driver's license rules in March that prohibited head coverings. The new rules were supposed to help law enforcement officers match people with their licenses.

Muslim women complained to Riley and legislators that their religion required them to wear a head scarf, or hijab, that covers their hair, ears and neck.

In response, the governor asked Coppage and King to review the complaints and see if changes could be made. King said the change in policy would also accommodate Roman Catholic nuns and people who are wearing head coverings after losing their hair due to cancer treatments.

People wearing a head covering for a medical reason must have a statement from a licensed physician in Alabama noting the medical condition.

Veils are not permitted under the revised policy.

Floyd complimented the governor for responding quickly to the women's complaints and not waiting until someone sued the state.

"When the governor saw that rule, he said, oh no, we've got to get that changed," she said. Ibrahim Hooper, spokesman for the Council on American-Muslim Relations in Washington, said the policy change brings Alabama in line with the majority of states.

Coppage cautioned that the rule change would not accommodate a common request from motorists who want their photos taken while wearing sunglasses. He said sunglasses and eye patches can only be worn for verified medical reasons.

Appendix E

MUSLIM STUDENT'S RIGHTS VIOLATED

By ASJYLYN LODER HERALD NEWS

Fairleigh Dickinson University in Teaneck violated the civil rights of a Muslim nursing student by ordering her to remove a religious head covering during nursing rounds at St. Mary's Hospital in Passaic, the state attorney general charged on Thursday.

"We are one nation that is indivisible by race or religion," said Attorney General Peter Harvey in a statement released Thursday. "Each of us is obliged to respect the beliefs, the dignity, and the customary practices of all religions. It is not only the right thing to do, it is the law."

University officials told the student—identified in legal documents as Debra Mason of Jersey City—that her head covering violated a school policy requiring nursing students to wear uniforms during clinical rounds, according to the Attorney General's Office. New Jersey law requires employers to make reasonable accommodations for religious customs, and the university policy violates that law, the office alleged.

"The university will respond to the findings in accordance with the procedures of the law against discrimination and beyond this we have no comment," said a spokesperson for the university.

Mason could not be reached for comment.

Mason enrolled in Fairleigh Dickinson's nursing program in May 2004, according to the Attorney General's Office. An introductory course required her to conduct three-day clinical rounds at St. Mary's Hospital. Nursing school officials told Mason that St. Mary's prohibited head covering during rounds, which the hospital denies.

"We have no such policy," said St. Mary's Hospital spokesman Lance Abramowitz. He said that hospital employees wear religious head coverings like head scarves and yarmulkes, as well as other articles of religious dress, like crucifixes.

Mason went without the head covering on two occasions before complaining to a nursing school professor that she felt uncomfortable not wearing it. Knowing that the issue would arise again the following semester, Mason attempted to broker a compromise by offering to wear a skullcap, but withdrew the offer after consulting with her husband and deciding the skullcap was not sufficient.

Rather than further compromise her religious beliefs, Mason withdrew from the nursing program.

"This is part of what some Muslims feel is how they should be dressed, and people need to respect that," said Sharine El-Abd, commissioner for the New Jersey Civil Rights Commission, an advisory group to the attorney general's civil rights division.

J. Frank Vespa-Papaleo, director of the attorney general's Division of Civil Rights, said this is the only such case he can recall in the past several years.

The Attorney General's Office issued a finding or probable cause Thursday, a legal step tantamount to a civil indictment.

The case now moves to a conciliation process.

If it is not resolved, it will be referred to the New Jersey Office of Administrative Law, where an administrative law judge will hold a hearing and issue a decision.

That process can take several months to a year or more, Vespa-Papaleo said.

While there has been a highly publicized French ban on Muslim head covering in that country's schools, Muslim anti-discrimination groups said such incidents are on the decline in the U.S. because advocates raised awareness about Muslim customs and about laws protecting religious practices.

"I think the situation in the workplace has improved tremendously.

When we first started doing this work, so many employers were just not aware of the law," said Ibrahim Hooper, spokesman for the Council on American-Muslim Relations, a Washington D.C. Muslim civil-rights and advocacy group.

CAIR publishes a series of $3 guides for educators, health care professionals and employers on Muslim religious practices, which can be purchased at t *www.cair-net.org*, or by calling (202) 488-8787.

Reach Asjylyn Loder at (973) 569-7158 or loder@northjersey.com.

Appendix F

MUSLIM WOMAN DENIED
JOB FOR SCARF SUES

06-03-2006   Associated Press:

A Muslim woman who claims she was denied employment after she refused to remove a head scarf worn for religious reasons is accusing a Des Moines convenience store chain of violating her religious rights.

In the lawsuit, Aaliyah Withers-Johnson claims officials at Git-N-Go Convenience Stores Inc. told her she could not work for the company if she insisted on wearing the head scarf, known as a hijib, worn as part of her Muslim faith.

The lawsuit, filed in U.S. District Court in Des Moines, accuses the company of racial and religious discrimination.

Withers-Johnson, who also is black, claims she wore the scarf to her initial job interview for a position as a store clerk on March 11, 2005, was offered a position and told to report six days later for training.

But at the training session, Withers-Johnson claims she was immediately pulled aside by a company official and told she would not be able to start "because of the thing you are wearing on your head," the lawsuit said.

Officials say company policy prohibits employees from wearing caps, scarves or anything on their head.

Withers-Johnson told the official the scarf was required as part of her faith then asked if she was not being hired because of it, the lawsuit said.

The officials responded by saying: "If I let you wear it then everyone else is going to want to," according to the lawsuit.

"It shows that not everyone is always as sensitive as they need to be to people's religious beliefs," said Jill Zwagerman, the woman's attorney. "Her general reaction was pretty obvious when her religious attire was compared to a baseball cap or a scarf."

Withers-Johnson, who is a U.S. citizen and student at Drake University, is seeking an unidentified amount for lost wages and benefits and punitive damages.

She also wants a judge to bar the company from future discrimination of race-based stereotypes, require sensitivity training throughout the company and impose mandatory race bias testing on upper management officials.

The telephone message left Monday for attorneys for Git-N-Go wasn't immediately returned. The company operates as many as 38 stores in the Des Moines area.

Appendix G

MUSLIM GIRLS FIND SOLIDARITY TOGETHERNESS IN TROOP 1101

Paper: Charlotte Observer, The (NC)
Title: MUSLIM GIRLS FIND SOLIDARITY TOGETHERNESS IN
    TROOP 1101 IS A COMFORT, ESPECIALLY AMID TAUNTS
    AND MISUNDERSTANDING
Author: ANN DOSS HELMS, STAFF WRITER Date: October 2,
    2001
Section: FAMILY Page: 1E

As three police cars stood watch outside, Girl Scout Troop 1101 opened its recent meeting with a prayer and the Scout promise:

"On my honor, I will try to serve God and my world" Most Girl Scouts say "country" instead of "world." Most pray in English, not Arabic. But this Charlotte troop, where girls wear Scout sashes over their shoulders and scarves over their heads, has never been typical.

For six years it's been a second home for girls approaching adolescence in a culture at odds with their Muslim faith. They don't date, don't wear swimsuits, don't bare their arms and legs, even when they play sports.

At their schools, scattered through the Charlotte area, they're lucky if one or two other girls dress like they do. In the scout troop led by "Auntie" Rose Hamid, they never have to explain themselves.

"We are family!" 10-year-old Kulsum Ahmed proclaims, beaming.

Since Sept. 11, that sense of security has grown more precious. Before, their distinctive hijab, or covering for Muslim modesty, brought questions such as "Are you bald?"—annoying at times, but not malicious.

Now, a few students who associate Muslim appearance with terrorists call out, "Go back to where you came from!"

"I came from Connecticut," 10-year-old Sumaya Suleiman notes wryly. Identity is no simple matter, though. These girls—about 15 of them, ages 10 to 14—are Americans, but they have family ties to Pakistan, Palestinian territory, India, Somalia, Jordan and Chile. Their religion teaches that they are part of a world community of believers, more important than nationality—thus, the revision of the Girl Scout promise.

Now Islam is in the world spotlight, but these girls, like Muslims across the country, worry the attention is bringing more confusion than understanding.

"We don't even know any terrorists," says 13-year-old Kawthar Suleiman, Sumaya's sister. "We don't believe in blowing up stuff. Islam is not terrorist."

Many of the girls say American news media are overplaying the Muslim connection to the terrorists, even fabricating reports to make it look as if Muslims around the world are rejoicing.

They warily watch news of Americans attacking mosques, Muslims and people who look Middle Eastern.

Just after the terrorist attack, threats were phoned in to Charlotte mosques; that's why three squad cars sat outside the Muslim Society of Greater Charlotte on a recent Sunday, when the Scout meeting and other events took place. The society just built a new mosque and had a grand opening festival scheduled for late September; it was postponed for fear of attracting unwanted attention.

"If we celebrate anything, they'll think we're celebrating for the terrorists," says Reem, 14. The girls say they get tired of hearing about the attacks, especially when discussions bring misinformation or stereotypes. Ruhi says one of her teachers told the class that Muslims believe killing Christians is a direct route to heaven; Reem shook her head silently. Later, her mother called the teacher to say that just isn't true.

Despite the strain, daily life goes on. The girls still giggle at their meetings, still plan camping trips and fund-raisers. The Girl Scout Council has asked the girls to do a program on their faith for other troops this fall, as they have in the past.

Meanwhile, Hamid, the troop leader, goes through her own struggles. The mother of three, she is a flight-attendant trainer for US Airways. She grieves for all the attack victims, including flight crews. Her heart aches for coworkers losing their jobs in the aftermath.

And she grapples with complex questions of religion and world politics, seeking answers for herself and her troop. She tries to explain the complexities of jihad, or holy war, and cautions them against stereotyping non-Muslim Americans the way some are stereotyping Muslims.

"You've got these few idiots," she tells the troop, "just like these few idiot Muslims or those few idiots like Timothy McVeigh."

Ann Doss Helms: (704) 358-5033, *ahelms@charlotteobserver.com*

Appendix H

BOOKLIST

The following are a list of books that I have compiled which are suitable for school libraries. JUVENILE

1) Alta, C. (1995). *Allah Created Everything.* Amica Publishing House. ISBN: 1-884187-09-9

2) Child, J. (1995). *The Rise of Islam.* Peter Bedrick Books. ISBN: 0-87226-116-6

3) El-Moslimany, A. P. (1994). *Zaki's Ramadhan Fast.* Amica Publishing House. ISBN: 1-884187-080

4) Ghazi, S. H. (1996). *Ramadan.* Holiday House. ISBN: 0-8234-1254-7

5) Hoyt-Goldsmith, D. (2001). *Celebrating Ramadan.* Holiday House. ISBN:0-8234-1581-3 (hardcover) 0-8234-1762-x (paperbk)

6) Khan, A. K. (2003). *What You Will See Inside A Mosque.* Jewish Lights Publisher. ISBN: 1-893361-60-8

7) Khan, R. (2002). *Muslim Child. Understanding Islam Through Stories and Poems*. Albert Whitman and Company.
    ISBN: 0-8075-5307-7

8) Kyuchukov, H. (2004). *My Name Was Hussein*. Boyd Hills Press.
    ISBN: 1-56397-964-0

9) MacMillan, D. M. (1994). *Ramadan and Id al-Fitr*. Enslow Elementary; Library Binding Edition.
    ISBN: 0-89490-502-3

10) Marchant, K. (1998). *Id-ul-Fitr*. Millbrook Press.
    ISBN: 0-76130963-2

11) Oppenheim, S. L. (1994). *Iblis*. Harcourt Brace & Company.
    ISBN: 0-15-238016-7

12) Senker, C. (2004). *My Muslim Year*. Hodder Wayland.
    ISBN: 0-7502-4052-0

13) Tames, R. (1995). *Muslim. Beliefs and Cultures*. Franklin Watts Ltd.
    ISBN: 0-516-08078-4

14) Teece, G. (1998). *Religion in Focus. Islam*. Massachussetts: Paraclete Press.
    ISBN: 1-58340-467-8

15) Wallace, H. (2006). *Islam. This is my Faith*. Barron's Education Series.
    ISBN: 13: 978-0-7641-5966-4 (hardcover) 13:978-0-7641-3475-3 (paperbk)

16) Wilkinson, P. (2004). *Islam*. Darling Kindersley Publishers Ltd.
    ISBN: 0-7894-8870-1 (plc) 0-7894-8871-x (alb)

17) Wood, A. (2000). *Muslim Mosque*. Gareth Stevens Publishing.
    ISBN: 0-8368-2609-4

YOUNG ADULT

1) Abdel-Fattah, R. (2007). *Does My Head Look Big In This?* Orchard Books.
ISBN: 978-0-439-91947-0

2) Abdul Rauf, F. (2004). *What's Right With Islam?* Harper One.
ISBN: 0-06-058272-3

3) Aboulela, L. (2005). *Minaret*. Grove Press.
ISBN: 0-8021-7014-5

4) Akbar, S. H. (2005). *Come Back to Afghanistan*. Bloomsbury.
ISBN: 13:978-1-58234-520-8

5) Clinton, C. (2002). *A Stone in my Hand*. Candlewick.
ISBN: 0-7636-1388-6

6) Dardess, G. *Meeting Islam. A Guide for Christians.* Massachussetts: Paraclete Press.
ISBN: 1-55725-433-8

7) Diamond, A. (1994). *Malcolm X. A Voice for Black America.* Enslow Publishers.
ISBN: 0-89490-435-3

8) Emerick, Y. (2002). *Muhammad*. Alpha.
ISBN: 0-02-864371-2

9) Ernst, C. W. (1999). *Teachings of Sufism*. Shambhala.
ISBN: 1-57062-349-x

10) Stolz, J. (2004). *The Shadows of Ghadames*. Delacorte Books.
ISBN: 0-385-73104-3 (trade) 0-385-90131-3 (glb)

11) Haneef, S. (1995). *What Everyone Should Know About Islam and Muslims*. Kazi Publications.
ISBN: 0-935782-00-1

12) Kahf, M. (2003). *E-mails from Scheherazad.* University Press of Florida.
ISBN: 0-8130-2620-2 (cloth) 0-8130-2621-0 (pbk)

13) Nomani, A. (2005). *Standing Alone in Mecca.* Harper One.
ISBN: 0-06-057144-6

14) Riverband. (2005). *Baghdad Burning.* The Feminist Press CUNY.
ISBN: 1-55861-489-3

15) Sayres, M. N. (2006). *Anahita's Woven Riddle.* Amulet.
ISBN: 13:978-0-8109-5481-6 or 10:0-8109-5481-8

16) Yuan, M. S. (Editor). (2005). *Women in Islam.* Thomas Gale.
ISBN: 0-7377-2759-4

Book list suggested by the author Rukhsana Khan

1.	Al-Gailani, Noorah	The Muslim Year: Surahs, Stories and Celebrations (Hawthorn, 2003)
2.	Budhos, Marina	Ask Me No Questions (S & S, 2006)
3.	Bunting, Eve	One Green Apple (Clarion, 2006) (Viking, 2003)
4.	Canover, Sarah & Crane Freda	Ayat Jamila: Beautiful Signs (EWU, 2004)
5.	Demi	Muhammad (S & S, 2003)
6.	Ellis, Deborah	a) Parvana's Journey b) Mud City (Groundwood, 2003)

7. Emerick, Yahya — Ahmad Deen and the Jinn at Shaolin (Amirah, 1996)

8. English, Karen — Nadia's Hands (Boyd Mill, 2005)

9. Heide, Florence Parry — Sami and the Time of Troubles (Clarion, 1992)

10. Hoffman, Mary — The Color of Home (Putnam, 2002)

11. Hutchison, H.U. — Invincible Abdullah

(American Trust) * Series similar to the Hardy Boys

12. Khan, Rukhsana — The Roses in my Carpets (Fitzhenry & Whiteside, 2004)

Silly Chicken (Viking, 2005)

Ruler of the Courtyard (Viking, 2005)

Darling if You Luv me Would You Please Smile (Stoddard, 1999)

Muslim Child: Understanding Islam through Poems and Stories (Albert Whitman, 2002)

13. Laird, Elizabeth   A Little Piece of Ground
                                        (Macmillan, 2004) Kiss the
                                        Dust (Puffin, 1994)

14. Mellings, O.R.   My Blue Country (Viking,
                                        1996)

15. Mobin Uddin, Asma   My name is Bilal (Boyd
                                        Mills, 2005)

16. Nye, Naomi Shihab   Sitti's Secrets (S & S, 1994)
                                        Habibi (S & S, 1997)

17. Simpson, J.J.L   The Jinn in the Clock
                                        (American Trust, 1990)

18. Winter, Jeanette & Stamaty,
    Mark Alan
    The Librarian of Basra:
    A True Story from Iraq   (Harcourt, 2005)

    Alia's Mission: Saving
    the Books of Iraq   (Knopf, 2004)

Glossary

Adab—Good manners, proper etiquette.

Allah—Lord, Creator, God.

As Salamu Alaykum—Peace be upon you.

Ayat—Verse

Chaddah—Fabric that is worn as a body covering worn over the head and draped over one shoulder.

Deen—Religion

Fana—Annihilation

Hajj—Pilgrimage to the holy places in Mecca and its environs that every Muslim should make in their lifetime if they are financially and physically able to do so.

Hijab—Comes from the root word hadjaba meaning to conceal or hide from view.

Iman—To have faith in something and to proclaim it.

Islam—The way of life for Muslims.

Jalbab—A covering or garment usually worn over a female's pants and blouse or dress.

*Alternate spelling (jilbab) and also known as burka or burqa.

Jum'aa—The Friday religious observance that is incumbent upon men. It includes both a speech and prayer.

Kalimah—Testification that there is One God, and that Muhammad (PBUH) is his prophet and messenger.

Khamees—A knee length garment traditionally with slits up to the lower hips on both sides.

MABPWH—May Allah be pleased with her.

Mahdjub—Veiled (as in a spiritual veil).

Muhajaba—A female that wears hijab.

Muhajabat—Plural for muhajaba.

Muslim—One who submits to the will of God.

PBUH—Peace Be Upon Him. Used after mentioning the name of the Holy Prophet (PBUH) to convey respect.

Qadri Order—A branch of the sufi order founded by Sheikh Abdul Qadir Gilani (May Allah bless him).

Qur'an—The Holy Book revered by Muslims and revealed to the Prophet Muhammad (PBUH), through the Angel Gabriel.

Salaams—Peace

Salaat—Prayer

Saum—Fasting

Shalwar—Loose fitting pants.

Sheikh—Scholar

Sheikh el Islam—Scholar of the religion of Islam.

Sunnah—The way in which the Prophet lived and the examples he left behind.

Sunni—Followers of the Sunnah or the path of the Prophet (PBUH).

Surah—Chapter (referring to chapters in the Holy Qur'an).

Ummah—The followers of the Prophet Muhammad (PBUH). Wa Alaykum

Salaam—And peace be upon you.

Wahdiyaat—Oneness.

Zakat—Monetary tax that all Muslims should pay to benefit the poor or those less fortunate than themselves.

References

Akeret, R. U. (2000). *Photolanguage. How photos reveal the fascinating stories of our lives and relationships.* New York, New York: W.W. Norton & Company.

Abdarahman, A. & Johnson, Y. (1982). *Al-Muwatta. Imam Malik.* Cambridge, Great Britain: University Press.

Ali, M. (1993). *A Manual of Hadith.* Lahore, Pakistan: Anjuman Ishaat Islam.

Ali, S. (2005) Why here, why now? Young Muslim women wearing hijab. *The Muslim World.* 95, 473-614.

Atkinson, D. R., Morten, G., Sue, D. W. (1998). *Counseling American Minorities.* Boston, Massachusetts: McGraw Hill.

ASCD. (1977). *Encouraging multicultural education.* Grant, Carl (Editor). Multicultural Education: Commitments, issues and applications. Washington, D.C.: ASCD Publications.

Barron, L. (1994). *Focus on scarf styling.* Gatesville, South Africa: Hidden Treasure Press. Blair, M. & Holland, J. (Editors). (1995). *Identity and diversity.* Khanum, S. Education and the Muslim girl. Clevedon, England: Multilingual Matters.

Bullock, K. (2002). Rethinking Muslim women and the veil: Challenging historical and modern stereotypes. Herndon, Virginia: The International Institute of Muslim Thought.

Bryman, A. & Burgess, R. (Editors). (1999). *Qualitative research*. Volume I. London, England: Sage Publications.

CAIR. (2004). Alabama Muslims denied right to Muslim attire. *www. cair- net.org/asp/article.asp?id=158&page=AA*

Chaudhry, L. N. (2005). Aisha and her multiple identities: Excerpts from ethnographic encounters. *The Muslim World*. 95, 531-556. Hartford, Conneticut: Blackwell Publishing Company.

Collins, R. (1988). *Theoretical continuities in Goffman's work*. Drew, P. & Wootton, A. (Editors). Erving Goffman. Exploring the Interaction Order. Boston, Massachusetts: Northeastern University Press.

Cooke, M. (2001). *Muslim Women Claim Islam*. United Kingdom: Routledge.

Cruz, M. E. (1999). Preparing ourselves for a millenium of diversity, or enjoying the whole enchilada, collard greens, fry bread, and apple pie. *English Journal*. 88, pp. 16-18.

Deegan, M. J. (1987). *Symbolic interaction and the study of women: An introduction*. Deegan, M. J. & Hill, M. R. (Editors). Women and symbolic interaction. Winchester, Massachussetts: Allen & Unwin Inc.

Dei, G., Mazzuca, J., McIsaac, E. & Zine, J. (1997). *Reconstructing 'drop-out'*. Toronto, Canada: University of Toronto Press.

Donzel, E.J. (1971). *Hidjab*. Lewis, B., Menage, V.L., Pellat, C.H. & Schacht, J. (Editors). The encyclopedia of Islam, Volume III. London, England: Luzac & Company.

Du Bois, J.W. (2003). *Discourse and grammar*. Tomasello, M. (Editor). The new psychology of language. Mahwah, New Jersey: Lawrence Erlbaum Associates, Publishers.

Eder, D. & Fingerson, L. (2002). *Interviewing children and adolescents.* Gubrium, J. & Holstein, J. (Editors). Handbook of interview research. Thousand Oaks, California: Sage Publications.

El-Guindi, F. (1999). *Veil. Modesty, Privacy, and Resistance.* New York, New York: Berg.

Elias, Jamal J. (1998). *Death before dying. The Sufi poems of Sultan Bahu.* Berkeley, California: University of California Press.

Esposito, J. L. (2000). *Muslims in America or American Muslims.* Haddad, Y. Y. & Esposito, J. L. (Editors). Muslims on the Americanization Path? pp. 3-15. New York, New York: Oxford University Press.

Foeman, A. K. & Nance, T. (1999). From miscegenation to multiculturalism. perceptions and stages of interracial relationship development. *Journal of Black Studies.* 29, pp. 540-557. London, England: Sage Publications, Inc.

Gall, J., Gall, M.D., & Borg, W. (1999). *Applying educational research.* New York, New York: Addison Wesley Longman, Inc.

Garrison, J. (2002). *James's metaphysical pluralism, spirituality, and overcoming blindness to diversity in education.* Garrison, J., Podeschi, R. & Bredo, E. (Editors). William James and education. New York, New York: Teachers College Press.

Ghayur, M. A. (1981). *Muslims in the United States: Settlers and visitors.* Lambert, Richard (Editor). The Annals of The American Academy of Political and Social Science. Washington, D.C.: Georgetown University Press.

Goffman, E. (1963). *Behavior in public places. Notes on the social organization of gatherings.* Berkeley, California: Collier-Macmillan Ltd.

Goffman, E. (1961). *Encounters. Two studies in the sociology of interaction.* Indianapolis, Indiana: Bobbs-Merrill Educational Publishing.

Goffman, E. (1967). *Interaction ritual. Essays in face-to-face behavior.* Chicago, Illinois: Aldine Publishing Company.

Goffman, E. (1963). *Stigma. Notes on the management of spoiled identity.* New York, New York: Simon & Schuster Inc.

Haddad, Y. Smith, J. & Moore, K. (2006). *Muslim women in America.* New York, New York: Oxford University Press

Hanifi, M. A. (1980). *A survey of Muslim institutions and culture.* Lahore, Pakistan: Ashraf Printing Press.

Hallet, T. (2003). Emotional feedback and amplification in social interaction. *The Sociological Quarterly.* 44, 705-726. Berkeley, California: University of California Press.

Hasan, A. (1990). *Sunan Abu Dawud, Volume III.* New Delhi, India: Kitab Bhavan.

Haw, K. (1998). *Educating Muslim Girls.* Philadelphia, Pennsylvania: Open University Press.

Headley, C. (2002). *Postmodernism, narrative, and the question of black identity.* Birt, R. (Editor), Critical Essays in Africana Philosophy 45-71. Lanham, Maryland: Rowman & Littlefield Publishers, Inc.

Hekman, S. (1999). *Feminism, Identity, and Difference.* Portland, Oregon: Frank Cass Publishers.

Hermansen, M. K. (1991). *Two-way acculturation: Muslim women in America between individual choice (liminality) and community affiliation (communities).* Haddad, Y. (Editor). The Muslims of America. New York: New York, Oxford University Press.

Hewitt, J. P. (1997). *Self and society. A symbolic interactionist social psychology.* Needham Heights, Massachussetts: Allyn & Bacon.

Hudson-Weems, C. (1998). *Africana womanism.* Nnameka, O. (Editor). Sisterhood, feminisms and power: From Africa to the diaspora 149-160. Asmara, Eritrea: African World Press, Inc.

Jasser, G. (1999, September). The twin evils of the veil. *Social Identities.* 5, 1. 31-45. London, England: Carfax Publishing, Ltd.

Jilani, S. M. (1983). *Rauza-Tus-Safa. The life of Muhammad, messenger of Allah.* Lahore, Pakistan: Zavia Books.

Jones, C., (1986). *The study of spirituality.* Wainwright, G. & Yarnold, E. (Editors). New York, New York: Oxford University Press

Kahf, M. (2006). *The girl in the tangerine scarf.* New York, New York: Carroll & Graf Publishers.

Keltner, D., Young, R. C. & Buswell, B. N. (1997). Appeasement in human emotion, social practice, and personality. *Aggressive Behavior.* 23, 359-374. Berkeley, California: Wiley-Liss, Inc.

Kendon, A. (1988). *Goffman's approach to face-to-face interaction.* Drew, P. & Wootton, A. (Editors). Erving Goffman. Exploring the Interaction Order. Boston, Massachussetts: Northeastern University Press.

Khan, Dr. M. M. (1997). *The translation of the meanings of Sahih Al-Bukhari, volume* VII. Riyadh, Saudi Arabia: Darussalam Publishers and Distributors.

Khan, M.A. (2003). *Constructing the American Muslim community.* Haddad, Y., Smith, J. & Esposito, J. (Editors). *Religion and Immigration.* Christian, Jewish, and Muslim experiences in the United States. Lanham, Maryland: Rowman & Littlefield Publishers.

Khan, M. W. (Editor). (1981). *Education and society in the Muslim world.* Jeddah, Saudi Arabia: Hodder and Stoughton, Ltd.

Khan, R. (2006). Muslims in children's books. *School Library Journal*, *52, 36-37.*

Khan, S. (2000). *Muslim women. Crafting a North American identity.* Gainesville, Florida: University of Florida Press.

Kondo, D. K. (1990). *Crafting selves.* Chicago, Illinois: The University of Chicago Press.

Kinney, D. A., Rosier, K. B. & Harger, B. D. (2003). *The Educational Institution.* Reynolds, L. & Herman-Kinney, N. (Editors). Handbook of Symbolic Interactionism. Walnut Creek, California: Altamira Press.

Landorf, H. & Pagan, L. (2005, July/August). Unveiling the hijab. *Social Studies.* 96, 4. 171-177. Washington, DC: Heldref Publications.

Lantieri, L. (2001). *A vision of schools with spirit.* Lantieri, L. (Editor). Schools with spirit. Boston, Massachusetts: Beacon Press.

LeCompte, M. & Schensul, J. (1999). *Analyzing & interpreting ethnographic data.* Walnut Creek, California: AltaMira Press.

Lings, M. (1983). *Muhammad. His life based on the earliest sources.* Rochester, Vermont: Inner Traditions International, Ltd.

Lynch, J. (1987). *Prejudice reduction and the schools.* New York, New York: Nichols Publishing Company.

Madani, Dr. M. (1995). *Hijab.* Alexandria, Virginia: Al-Saadawi Publications.

Marulis, L. (2000). Anti-bias teaching to address cultural diversity. *Multicultural Education.* 7, 3, 27-31.

Mason, J. (1996). *Qualitative researching.* London, England: Sage Publications. Maxwell, J. (1996). *Qualitative research design.* Thousand Oaks, California: SAGE Publications.

Mead, G. H. (1982). *The individual and the social self.* Miller, D. (Editor). Chicago, Illinois: University of Chicago Press.

Mernissi, F. (1987). Beyond the veil. Bloomington, Indiana: Indiana University Press.

Miller, F. (1999). Understanding multicultural perspectives: A project approach. *Social Studies & Young Learner.* 11, 3, 22-23.

Minh-ha, T.T. (1988). Not you/like you: Post-Colonial women and the interlocking questions of identity and differences. *Inscriptions, 3 / 4,* 371-375.

Morris, D. (1977). *Manwatching. A field guide to human behavior.*

New York, New York: Harry N. Abrams, Inc.

Nevin, Rev. A., Horne, Rev. T. & Munroe, Rev. Wm H. (1875). *The Holy Bible containing the Old and New Testament.* Philadelphia, Pennsylvania: A.J. Holman & Co.

Noddings, N. (1984). *Caring. A feminine approach to ethics & moral education.* Berkeley, California: University of California Press.

Noddings, N. (2002). *Educating moral people. A caring alternative to character education.* New York, New York: Teachers College Press.

Nurbakhsh, Dr. J. (1983). *Sufi women.* New York, New York: Khaniqahi Nimatullahi Publications.

Pullen, P. (2000). Breaking racial stereotypes by reconstructing multicultural education. *Multicultural Education.* 7, 3, 44-46.

Rahman, F. (1996). *"Islam's origin and ideals".* Barazangi, N., Zaman, R.M. & Afzal O. (Editors). Muslim Identity and the Struggle for Justice. Gainesville, Florida: University of Florida Press.

Reynolds, L. T. & Herman-Kinney, N. J. (Editors). (2003). *Handbook of symbolic interactionism.* Walnut Creek, California: AltaMira Press.

Rice, P.L. & Ezzy, D. (1999). *Qualitative research methods.* Victoria, Australia: Oxford University Press.

Roald, A. S. (2000). Women in Islam. The western experience. New York, New York: Routledge.

Robson, J. (1964). *Mishkat Al-Masabih.* Lahore, Pakistan: SH. Muhammad Ashraf Publisher—Kashmiri Bazar.

Rock, P. (1999). *Participant observation.* Bryman, A. & Burgess, R. (Editors). Qualitative Research. Volume II. London, England: Sage Publications.

Ryen, A. (2002). *Cross-cultural interviewing.* Gubrium, J. & Holstein, J. (Editors). Handbook of Interviews Research. Thousand Oaks, California: Sage Publications.

Sarroub, L. K. (2005). *All American Yemeni girls. Being Muslim in a public school.* Philadelphia, Pennsylvania: University of Pennsylvania Press.

Schensul, S., Schensul, J. & LeCompte, M. (1999). *Essential ethnographic methods.* Walnut Creek, California: AltaMira Press.

Seidman, I. (1998). *Interviewing as qualitative research.* New York, New York: Teachers College Press.

Shah, I. (1970). *The way of the Sufi.* New York, New York: E.P. Dutton. Shaikh, S. (2003). *Transforming feminisms: Islam, women, and gender justice.* Safi, Omid (Editor). Progressive Muslims. On Justice, Gender, and Pluralism. Oxford, England: Oneworld Publications.

Shakeri, E. (2000). *"Muslim women in Canada. Their role and status as revealed in the hijab controversy".* Haddad, Y. & Esposito, J. L. (Editors). Muslims on the Americanization path? New York, New York: Oxford University Press.

Shilling, C. (1999). Towards an embodied understanding of the structure/agency relationship. *British Journal of Sociology.* 50, 4, 543-562. London, England: Taylor & Francis, Ltd.

Shonfeld-Ringel, S. (2001). A re-conceptualization of the working alliance in cross-cultural practice with non-western clients: Integrating relational perspectives and multicultural theories. *Clinical Social Work Journal.* 29, 1, 53-64. New York, New York: Human Sciences Press, Inc.

Sleeter, C. E. (2001). *An analysis of the critiques of multicultural education.* Banks, J. A. (Editor). Handbook of research on multicultural education. San Francisco, California: Jossey-Bass Inc. Publishers.

Sleeter, C. E. & Grant, C. A. (1999). *Making choices for multicultural education.* New York, New York: John Wiley & Sons, Inc.

Smagorinsky, P. & Taxel, J. (2005). *The discourse of character education. Culture wars in the classroom.* Mahwah, New Jersey: Lawrence Erlbaum Associates, Publishers.

Smith, M. (1974). *Rab'ia the mystic and her fellow-saints in Islam.* Amsterdam, The Netherlands: Philo Press.

Tariq, Maulana A. R. (1966). *Translation of Holy Qur'an.* Lahore, Pakistan: M. Siraj-ud-Din & Sons.

Tatum, B. (1997). *Why are all the black kids sitting together in the cafeteria?* New York, New York: Basic Books.

Tisdell, E. (2003). *Exploring spirituality and culture in adult and higher education.* San Francisco, California: Jossey-Bass.

Ulen, E. N. (2005). *Tapping our strength.* Afzal-Khan, Fawzia (Editor). Shattering the Stereotypes. Muslim Women Speak Out. Northampton, Massachusetts: Olive Branch Press.

Vogelsang-Eastwood, G.M. (1996). *For modesty's sake?* The Netherlands: Syntax Publishers.

Vryan, K. D., Adler, P. A. & Adler, P. (2003). *Identity.* Reynolds, L. & Herman-Kinney, N. (Editors). Handbook of Symbolic Interactionism.Walnut Creek, California: Altamira Press.

Walker, A. (1983). *In search of our mother's gardens: Womanist prose.* New York, New York: Harcourt Brace Jovanovich.

Walker, R. (1999). *Finding a silent voice for the researcher: Using photographs in evaluation and research.* Bryman, A. & Burgess, R. (Editors). Qualitative Research, Volume II. Thousand Oaks, California: Sage Publications Inc.

Weiss, W. (2000). *Islam. An illustrated historical overview.* Hauppauge, New York: Barron's Educational Series, Inc.

West. C. (1995). *A matter of life and death.* Rajchman, J. (Editor). The identity in question. New York, New York: Routledge.

Zine, J. (2006). Unveiled Sentiments: Gendered Islamophobia and experiences of veiling among Muslim girls in a Canadian Muslim school. *Equity & Excellence in Education.* 39, 239-252.

www.ingramcontent.com/pod-product-compliance
Lightning Source LLC
Chambersburg PA
CBHW022247290526
45785CB00015B/374